Teaching Language as Communication

Teaching Language as Communication

H. G. Widdowson

Oxford University Press

Oxford University Press
Walton Street, Oxford OX2 6DP

Oxford New York Toronto
Delhi Bombay Calcutta Madras Karachi
Petaling Jaya Singapore Hong Kong Tokyo
Nairobi Dar es Salaam Cape Town
Melbourne Auckland

and associated companies in
Berlin Ibadan

Oxford, Oxford English, and the *Oxford English* logo are
trade marks of Oxford University Press

ISBN 0 19 437077 1

© H. G. Widdowson 1978

First published 1978
Eighth impression 1990

Set in Monotype Imprint

Printed in Hong Kong

To my father, G. P. Widdowson

Contents

Introduction

This book is an attempt to clarify certain issues that seem to me to arise from adopting a communicative approach to the teaching of language. I have in mind, in particular, the teaching of English to speakers of other languages. Over recent years I (and a number of others) have advocated such an approach in principle and have tried to put it into practice in the preparation of teaching materials. In principle and practice, however, there always seemed to be loose ends of one sort or another: inconsistencies, unexamined assumptions, unresolved difficulties. My aim in this book was to sort out some of the things that I had been saying, consider their implications more closely, and see if they might be ordered into a coherent account. I wanted to try to think things through.

The 'communicative' approach is, of course, very much in vogue at present. As with all matters of fashion, the problem is that popular approbation tends to conceal the need for critical examination. There seems to be an assumption in some quarters, for example, that language is automatically taught as communication by the simple expedient of concentrating on 'notions' or 'functions' rather than on sentences. But people do not communicate by expressing isolated notions or fulfilling isolated functions any more than they do so by uttering isolated sentence patterns. We do not progress very far in our pedagogy by simply replacing abstract isolates of a linguistic kind by those of a cognitive or behavioural kind. If we are seriously interested in an approach to language teaching which will develop the ability to communicate, then we must accept the commitment to investigate the whole complex business of communication and the practical consequences of adopting it as a teaching aim. Such a commitment involves, I believe, a consideration of the nature of discourse and of the abilities that are engaged in creating it. This is the main concern of the first part of this book. The commitment involves, too, an attempt to think out the possible pedagogic procedures which will lead the learner towards the ability to handle discourse. The second part of the book represents such an attempt. I do not claim that in either part I have done any more than open up a number of possibilities. Our present state of knowledge about language and language learning is such that it would be irresponsible to be anything but tentative. But it would be even more irresponsible to avoid investigation and to pretend that there are no problems.

So this book is not in any way intended as propaganda for a new 'communicative' orthodoxy in language teaching. It is, on the contrary, an appeal for critical investigation into the bases of a belief and its practical implications. I am not trying to present a conclusive case but to start an inquiry.

There are, it seems to me, two ways of looking at publication. The first, which one might dub the classical view, regards appearance in print as the final public revelation of carefully rehearsed ideas made as definitive and as precise as possible. The aim is for universality and permanence and one proceeds towards publication with cautious circumspection. This classical view is the one expressed by Alexander Pope in his curt recommendation to other, and lesser, poets: 'Keep your piece nine years!' The other view, the romantic, is less concerned with completeness, is much less cautious and circumspect, and regards publication, more cavalierly perhaps, as a device for public speculation. The aim here is to stimulate interest by exposure, to suggest rather than to specify, to allow the public access to personal thinking. It is this second view that I subscribe to in publishing this book. I accept, therefore, that its contents are transitional and transient. They are meant as a personal consideration of issues that seem to me to stand in need of examination at the moment.

When I say that this book is personal, I do not want to imply that I have produced it in isolation from the ideas of others. Quite the reverse. Over the past eight years I have had the benefit of continuing discussions with the staff and students in the Department of Linguistics at Edinburgh and most of what is worthwhile in this book derives directly or indirectly from them. Now, as I am about to leave Edinburgh for London, I should like to express my sense of personal and professional debt to that department. I must make particular mention of Patrick Allen with whom I have worked in developing the *English in Focus* series, which has been, and continues to be, an attempt to produce practical teaching materials in accordance with the kind of approach I explore here. The authors of particular titles in the series—Eric Glendinning, Elizabeth Laird, Joan Maclean, Alan Mountford and Ian Pearson—have all made valuable contributions to this development and have given me ideas that I would not have thought of on my own. Other people whose influence I would particularly like to acknowledge are Tony Howatt, who was kind enough to read through an earlier draft of the book and made many valuable suggestions for improvement, Guy Aston, Christopher Candlin, Malcolm Coulthard, John Sinclair, Hugh Trappes-Lomax, Sandy Urquhart and David Wilkins. None of these people will agree with everything I say, of course; some might be quite appalled at the effect of their influence; all of them would very likely have made a better job of various parts of this book.

A different kind of influence altogether has been that of my wife. It is equally important, although I do not acknowledge it openly as often as I ought.

H. G. Widdowson
Edinburgh
March 1977

1 Usage and use

1.1 Correctness and appropriacy

The aims of a language teaching course are very often defined with
reference to the four 'language skills': understanding speech, speaking,
reading and writing. These aims, therefore, relate to the kind of activity
which the learners are to perform. But how can we characterize this
activity? What is it that learners are expected to understand, speak,
read and write? The obvious answer is: the language they are learning.
But what exactly do we mean by this? We might mean a selection of
lexical items recorded in a dictionary combined with syntactic structures
recorded in a grammar. In this view, the teaching of a language involves
developing the ability to produce correct sentences. Many teachers
would subscribe to this view and it has been productive of a good deal of
impressive language teaching material. In some respects, however, it is
unsatisfactory. We may readily acknowledge that the ability to produce sentences is a crucial one in the learning of a language. It is
important to recognize, however, that it is not the only ability that
learners need to acquire. Someone knowing a language knows more than
how to understand, speak, read and write sentences. He also knows how
sentences are used to communicative effect.

We may conveniently begin by considering an example of a correct
English sentence:

The rain destroyed the crops.

Here we have a correct English sentence and we might wish to say that
anybody speaking or writing such a sentence gives evidence of a good
knowledge of the language. We would judge anybody producing
the following sentences, on the other hand, to have an inadequate
knowledge:

The rain is destroy the crops.
The rain destruct the crops.

But what would we say if someone produced our correct sentence in the
following context?

(A approaches B, a stranger, in the street)
A: Could you tell me the way to the railway station, please?
B: The rain destroyed the crops.

The sentence remains correct, of course, but we might well hesitate to say that B had a good knowledge of English on this evidence. We would be inclined to say that he did not really know the language. It might be objected that nobody in his senses would ever seriously utter this sentence in response to the kind of question that A puts. But why not? The answer is that when we acquire a language we do not only learn how to compose and comprehend correct sentences as isolated linguistic units of random occurrence; we also learn how to use sentences appropriately to achieve a communicative purpose. We are not just walking grammars.

It might appear that the example I have given is somewhat extreme. Let us consider another:

A: What did the rain do?
B: The crops were destroyed by the rain.

This is a distinct improvement on the previous exchange, but as competent speakers of English we can recognize, nevertheless, that B's reply is still in some way the wrong kind of reply. It does not take on an appropriate form in this context. By the same token we recognize that the following are odd combinations of sentences:

A: What was destroyed by the rain?
B: The rain destroyed the crops.

A: What happened to the crops?
B: The rain destroyed the crops.

We also recognize that the following exchanges are quite normal:

A: What did the rain do?
B: It destroyed the crops.

A: What was destroyed by the rain?
B: The crops.

A: What happened to the crops?
B: They were destroyed by the rain.

Making an appropriate reply is a matter of selecting a sentence which will combine with the sentence used for asking the question. Or it may involve using only part of a sentence, as in the second of the normal exchanges given above.

1.2 Usage and use as aspects of performance

The learning of a language, then, involves acquiring the ability to compose correct sentences. That is one aspect of the matter. But it also involves acquiring an understanding of which sentences, or parts of sentences are appropriate in a particular context. The first kind of ability depends upon a knowledge of the grammatical rules of the language being learned. We can demonstrate this knowledge by producing strings of sentences without regard to context:

The rain destroyed the crops.
The cat sat on the mat.
The unicorn is a mythical beast.
Poor John ran away.
The farmer killed the duckling.
John loves Mary.
My tailor is rich.

To produce sentences like this is to manifest our knowledge of the language system of English. We will say that they are instances of correct English *usage*. But of course we are not commonly called upon simply to manifest our knowledge in this way in the normal circumstances of daily life. We are generally required to use our knowledge of the language system in order to achieve some kind of communicative purpose. That is to say, we are generally called upon to produce instances of language *use*: we do not simply manifest the abstract system of the language, we at the same time realize it as meaningful communicative behaviour.

This distinction between usage and use is related to de Saussure's distinction between *langue* and *parole* and Chomsky's similar distinction between competence and performance.[1] It is important to make clear what this distinction is. The notion of competence has to do with a language user's knowledge of abstract linguistic rules. This knowledge has to be put into effect as behaviour, it has to be revealed through performance. When it is put into effect through the citation of sentences to illustrate these rules, as is done in grammar books, then performance yields instances of usage: abstract knowledge is manifested. When language teachers select structures and vocabulary for their courses they select those items of usage which they judge to be most effective for teaching the underlying rules of the language system. Usage, then, is one aspect of performance, that aspect which makes evident the extent to which the language user demonstrates his knowledge of linguistic rules. Use is another aspect of performance: that which makes evident the extent to which the language user demonstrates his ability to use his knowledge of linguistic rules for effective communication.

In normal circumstances, linguistic performance involves the simultaneous manifestation of the language system as usage and its realization as use. But we can separate one from the other if we wish by focusing our attention on one rather than the other. When we are engaged in conversation we do not as a rule take note of such usage phenomena as grammatical irregularities (which may be quite frequent) in the speech of the person we are talking to, unless they force themselves on our attention by impeding communication. Our concern is with use and this concern filters out such irregularities of usage. If we assume the role of linguists in search of data, on the other hand, we might well adjust our focus of attention and concentrate on our interlocutor's usage, take note of his hesitations and repetitions, the peculiarites of his pronunciation and so on. The terms we have in English for referring to performance reflect these two aspects of behaviour. An expression like 'She speaks indistinctly', for example, refers to usage and an expression like 'He speaks persuasively' refers to use. I shall return to the relevance of the usage/use distinction to a definition of the so-called 'language skills' in Chapter 3.

Although there is a natural coincidence of usage and use in normal language behaviour, these two aspects of performance tend to be treated separately by people concerned with the description and the teaching of languages. Thus the grammarian illustrates the abstract rules of the system of the language he is describing by devising sentences in isolation which manifest these rules. The language teacher designing materials has also generally been inclined to concentrate on usage: the common practice is to select and organize language items with a view to demonstrating how the rules of the system can be manifested through sentences. There has been less concern with demonstrating how such rules can be realized for communicative purposes as use. So when the teacher introduces a sentence like:

A book is on the table.

he does so to manifest the operation of a set of rules for sentence formation. He is not offering it as an example of a meaningful act of communication. In fact, utterances of sentences of this kind are of relatively rare occurrence as instances of use.

1.3   Usage and use in classroom presentation

I want now to consider some examples of how language is presented in the classroom and how this presentation, in concentrating on usage, may sometimes involve an inappropriate use of language. The following is an example of a familiar oral drill in which the learner is required to repeat a sentence pattern by using different 'call-words'

Teacher:	Book
Pupils:	There is a book on the table.
Teacher:	Bag.
Pupils:	There is a bag on the table.

Teacher: Pen.
Pupils: There is a pen on the table.
Teacher: Under the table.
Pupils: There is a pen under the table.
Teacher: On the floor.
Pupils: There is a pen on the floor.

What is going on here? We have a series of responses to a verbal cue but these responses are not replies in any normal sense. The pupils are demonstrating their knowledge of usage by manipulating the sentence pattern but they are not doing so for any other purpose.

Let us now adjust the drill so that we get what appears to be a more normal question and answer sequence:

Teacher: What is on the table?
Pupils: There is a book on the table.
Teacher: What is on the floor?
Pupils: There is a bag on the floor.
Teacher: Where is the bag?
Pupils: The bag is on the floor.
Teacher: Where is the book?
Pupils: The book is on the table.

Here we can recognize that some account is taken of use. To begin with, for the pupils to give an answer there must be a book on the table and a bag on the floor: there must be some simple situation to refer to. The pupils are not simply spinning sentences out without any reference to what the words mean, as they are in the first drill. But although there is some concern for use in this respect, it is still usage which has the dominant emphasis. Although the pupils' response is a reply to a question and not just a reaction to a prompt, the *form* of the reply is inappropriate. We can compare the drill with the following exchanges where the replies take on a more normal appearance:

A: What is on the table?
B: A book.
A: Where is the bag?
B: On the floor.

Even in this form, however, the language cannot necessarily be regarded as demonstrating appropriate use. To see why this is so, we have to ask ourselves: 'Why does A ask this question?' If a book is seen to be on the table, and a bag seen to be on the floor, and if everybody is aware of the location of these objects, then why does A need to ask where they are? If there is a book on the table in front of the whole class, then, as has been pointed out, the question is contextualised to the extent that it refers to something outside language and is not just a manipulation of the language itself. But by the same token, the fact that there *is* a book on the table, visible to everybody, makes it extremely unnatural to ask if it is there. Thus the provision of a situation may lead away from usage in one respect but lead back to usage in another. Only if the pupils know that the teacher cannot see the bag and is genuinely looking for it does his question as to its whereabouts take on the character of natural use. The following classroom exchange, for example, would commonly take on this genuine quality of real communication:

Teacher: Where's the duster?
Pupils: Under your chair.

We may say that the realization of language as use involves two kinds of ability. One kind is the ability to select which form of sentence is appropriate for a particular *linguistic context*. The second is the ability to recognize which function is fulfilled by a sentence in a particular *communicative situation*. Let us look again at our examples.

Teacher: What is on the table?
Pupils: There is a book on the table.

If this is part of a drill and there is a book on the table which everybody can see, then the teacher's question is not fulfilling a normal function since in ordinary circumstances we do not ask questions about something we already know. So the teacher's question and the pupils' answer do not fulfil a communicative function in this particular situation. Furthermore, a question of this form does not normally require a response which takes the form of sentence which the pupils give, so their reply is not appropriate in this particular linguistic context. This exchange, then, illustrates both inappropriate function in relation to the situation and inappropriate form in relation to the context. Let us now consider a second example:

Teacher: What is on the table?
Pupils: A book.

In this case, we have a reply which is appropriate with regard to form. But the function of the question and answer sequence remains as unnatural as before: the situation is still the same and still makes the question and answer inappropriate. This becomes clear if we compare this last example with what can be taken as an instance of genuine language use like the following:

Teacher: Where's the duster?
Pupils: Under your chair.

or:

Teacher: Where's Mary today?
Pupils: She's not well.

Here, it is appropriate for the teacher to ask a question and for the pupils to answer him: the situation is that he doesn't know where his duster is, and he doesn't know where Mary is, and he supposes that his pupils might know. Furthermore, the pupils' reply takes on an appropriate form in each exchange.

We have considered the case where sentences may have the appropriate form in the context in which they appear but which nevertheless do not function appropriately in the situation. We can also have sentences which function appropriately but whose form does not seem to be entirely appropriate. Consider the following:

Teacher: Where's the duster?
Pupils: The duster is under your chair.
Teacher: Where's Mary today?
Pupils: Mary is not well today.

I should make it clear that it is not my intention to question the usefulness of drills of the kind that we have been discussing but only to point out what they are useful for. They can teach that aspect of use which has to do with appropriate contextual form. But in normal language behaviour this is inseparably bound up with that aspect of use involving situational function, which these drills commonly are not designed to accommodate.

Let us now consider other classroom procedures in the light of the usage/use distinction that has been made. One of them which might appear to introduce use is what is generally referred to as 'situational presentation'. This involves the teacher demonstrating meaning by reference to objects or events actually present or enacted in the classroom. These objects and events are said to represent the situation. Thus, for example, the teacher in the early stages of an English course might hold up a pen, point to it and say:

This is a pen.

Here we have a correct English sentence. It is an instance of correct usage. But is it also an instance of appropriate use? It is true that the sentence makes reference to something in the situation devised by the teacher. But the situation that he has devised is not one which would normally require him to make use of such a sentence. The pupils know what a pen is as an object. What they do not know is what this object is called in English. The sentence which the teacher produces is of the kind which would be appropriate if it were necessary to identify an object: his sentence would normally function as an identification. But the learners do not need to have the object *identified* as a pen, they need to have it *named* as 'a pen' (as opposed to 'une plume', 'ein Feder', or whatever other term is used in their own language). So the form of sentence which is needed if use is to be demonstrated is really something like:

The English word for this is 'pen'.

or:

This is called 'a pen' in English.

Notice that this does not mean that the structure exemplified by a sentence like 'This is a pen' cannot take on an appropriate communicative function in another situation. Imagine, for example, a chemistry laboratory. The teacher is showing his pupils a flask of liquid and for the purposes of the experiment he is about to carry out he needs to identify what it is. In this situation he can quite appropriately say:

This is sulphuric acid.

Here he is not just demonstrating a structure, he is using the language for a required communicative purpose.

Similarly, if the teacher has been talking about, say, barometers and then wants to make sure that his class knows what a barometer actually looks like before going on to demonstrate how it works, then he can present the instrument for their inspection and quite appropriately say:

This is a barometer.

In these cases, the sentence pattern we are considering takes on a natural function in the situation. It is not simply an instance of correct usage; it is also an instance of appropriate use.

Let us consider another example. One of the most widespread ways of demonstrating the present continuous tense by 'situational presentation' is for the teacher to perform an activity like walking to the door or the window and to say, while doing so,

I am walking to the door.
I am walking to the window.

Now although the teacher has thereby devised a situation which makes the meaning of his sentence plain, the situation at the same time makes his sentence inappropriate in terms of use. Since everybody sees him walking to the door and walking to the window there is no need whatever for him to announce that he is doing these things. The situation would not normally call for such a comment. If my wife, for example, leaves the room during a dinner party she does not say:

I am walking to the door.

What she *may* say is something like:

I am going to the kitchen to see if the dinner's ready.

But she will only say this if she thinks that some explanation is called for. Otherwise she will say nothing at all, or perhaps some thing like:

Excuse me for a moment. I must go to the kitchen.

and everybody will realize that she has to go to the kitchen to attend to the dinner.

One can, however, think of other situations in which an utterance of a sentence of the form we are considering would be appropriate as an instance of use. Imagine, for example, the situation in which one person is in a telephone box describing the movements of somebody else to a third person at the other end of the line. This kind of situation occurs fairly frequently in detective films. The person on the telephone might in this situation produce sentences like the following:

The suspect is crossing the road. He is talking to the newspaper seller on the corner.

In this case, these sentences are being used to provide a commentary for somebody who is not present at the scene. Similarly, we can think of the situation in which a bomb-disposal expert is giving a commentary on his actions as he dismantles an explosive device:

I am turning the red switch on the left of the dial. I am now disconnecting the right hand wire.

Here we have sentences used appropriately because people who cannot see what is going on (they have retired to a safe distance) need to know what the expert is doing. If he fails and the bomb explodes, the next expert will have some idea how to avoid the same fate.

The point that is being made here in citing these examples is that a sentence pattern of the kind exemplified by:

I am walking to the door.
He is walking to the door.
etc.

can function appropriately as an instance of use if the situation is such that in producing such a sentence the speaker is at the same time performing an act of communication, like explaining something or giving a commentary. In the case of an explanation, the speaker makes clear what he or she is doing, or what somebody else is doing, on the assumption that this is not self evident. In the case of a commentary, the speaker tells somebody else who is not present at the scene what is going on. These can be said to represent certain contextual conditions which determine that sentences of the form in question count as actual instances of use and not simply instances of usage. But in the case of the teacher saying a sentence of this kind while actually performing the activity referred to neither of these conditions holds: it is self-evident what he is doing and so no explanation is called for and everybody can see perfectly well what he is doing, so no commentary is called for either. The sentence being presented, therefore, is not so much an instance of use as an instance of usage. The language is being manifested but not realized as normal communicative behaviour.

1.4　Aspects of meaning: signification and value

Now when I say that in drills and in so-called 'situational presentation' what we very often have is a demonstration of usage rather than use, I do not mean to imply that these procedures are therefore necessarily to be avoided. But I think that it is important for us to be aware of their limitations. Nor do I want to say that the production of sentences like 'This is a pen' and 'I am walking to the door' are meaningless. They have meaning of a kind, but this meaning which attaches to usage is not the same as meaning which attaches to use. Consider again the odd little exchange that was discussed earlier in the chapter:

A: Could you tell me the way to the railway station, please?
B: The rain destroyed the crops.

Now we might wish to say that B's remark is meaningless, and indeed *as a reply*, as the communicative use of a sentence, it *is* meaningless. But it does not follow that it is meaningless *as a sentence*, that is to say as an instance of usage. If we know the dictionary meanings of the lexical items and understand the syntactic relations between them then we can recognize that this sentence represents a proposition and so has meaning in a way which the following collection of words does not:

the destroy rain crops the.

We could work out a meaning for ourselves by re-organizing the words and providing an appropriate verb form, that is to say by applying grammatical rules, but this would be to treat this collection of words as a puzzle to be deciphered. Since the words themselves do not as they stand constitute a sentence they do not signal a proposition, although of course each of the lexical words (*destroy, rain, crops*) has meaning as an individual semantic unit.

　　Are we to suppose, then, that if we come across a group of words which does not make up a sentence then this group does not form a unit of meaning? Consider the following:

The rain.
The rain did.

Neither of these groups of words constitutes a sentence, and when considered in isolation like this express no proposition. They differ radically from the random collection of words given earlier, however, in that they can occur as contextually appropriate forms which combine with a preceding sentence. For example:

A: What destroyed the crops?
B: The rain.

or:

B: The rain did.

These groups of words become meaningful in relation to the sentence produced by A and we recognize that they express the proposition 'The rain destroyed the crops'.

In view of what has been said, it would seem helpful to make a distinction between two kinds of meaning. Sentences have meaning as instances of usage: they express propositions by combining words into structures in accordance with grammatical rules. We will call this kind of meaning *signification*. The second kind of meaning is that which sentences and parts of sentences assume when they are put to use for communicative purposes. We will refer to this as *value*.

Using these terms, we can now say that the oddity of B's remark in the exchange we considered earlier (when A asked the way to the railway station) lies in the fact that although it has signification as a sentence, it has no recognizable value as an instance of use: we can make no sense of it as a reply to A's question. We can also say that the string of words:

the destroy rain crops the

has no significance taken together since it does not comprise a sentence, although each of the lexical words has a signification as an isolated vocabulary item. The case is somewhat different with regard to expressions like:

The rain.
The rain did.

Although these expressions have no signification as sentences, they take on value when they occur in the kind of context that was provided for them earlier.

I want now, as before, to relate this discussion to pedagogic issues by seeing how this distinction can be applied to certain language teaching procedures. The following sentences are of quite common occurrence in the early stages of English courses:

This is a nose.
This is my leg.
etc.

Having presented sentences like this in a demonstration, either by pointing to the relevant parts of his own anatomy or by using a picture, the teacher might go on to provide practice in manipulating these structures by getting his pupils to participate in question and answer sequences of the following sort:

Teacher: What's this?
Pupils: It's a nose.
Teacher: What's this?
Pupils: It's a leg
and so on.

This procedure can be effective in teaching the signification of structures like 'This is a . . .' and of various vocabulary items which can be introduced into the syntactic framework. But it will be readily accepted that sentences like 'This is a nose' are seldom used in actual communication. In this respect, their value as use is low. Furthermore, the teacher's question is not like a normal question: rather it is a prompt for the pupils to produce the required instance of usage. We cannot say that the exchange between teacher and pupils represents a normal instance of language use, but only that it is a teaching device to enable the pupils to establish the signification of a certain structure and certain words in their minds and to provide them with practice by repetition.

Although the teacher in a sense provides a situation to make these sentences meaningful in that he points to his own nose, or the nose of somebody in a picture, the situation is one which will only serve to indicate the kind of meaning which we have called signification. It is possible, however, to conceive of situations in which this sentence and others like it, and the question and answer sequence illustrated above, do take on appropriate value and therefore become instances of use. Imagine the situation, for example, of somebody trying to work out what a rather obscure picture is intended to represent, or of two people engaged on doing a jig-saw puzzle.[3] But the fact that it requires some ingenuity to think of situations which would serve to give value to sentences like 'This is a leg' and 'It's a nose' suggests that their *potential* value is rather low. The potential value of the interrogative sentence that the teacher uses here is, of course, much higher, even though this value is not realized in the classroom situation which has been described.

1.5   Usage and use in the design of language teaching materials

In what has just been said, a further distinction has been made between the potential value of a unit of language and the realization of this value in an actual instance of use. Let us look at this distinction more closely. In designing a language course, we select from a description of the language in question (as represented in grammars and dictionaries) those structures and words which we suppose will be of most use to the learner for the purposes for which he is learning the language. That is to say, we select items of the highest potential value: those which can be realized to perform the kinds of acts of communication which the learner will have to deal with. The different criteria usually appealed to in selection have been discussed in detail elsewhere[4] and there is no need to go into the matter here. It is important to stress, however, that from the point of view adopted in this chapter items would be selected not because they occur frequently as instances of usage but because they have a high potential occurrence as instances of use of relevance to the learner's purposes in learning. In fact, the reason why the criterion of frequency alone has been found to be insufficient for selection purposes is precisely because it reflects only usage. The criterion of coverage, on the other hand, relates not to usage but to potential use, as indeed does that of 'disponibilité', or availability.

Potential value, then is accounted for in the selection stage of the language teaching process. Realized value, on the other hand, has to do with the stage of grading and presentation. We will suppose, for example, that the structure 'This is . . .' has been selected for inclusion in a particular course on the grounds that it is commonly used to identify an object in the kind of communication the learners will ultimately have to deal with. That is to say, this particular structure takes on the value of an identifying statement. Let us also suppose that it has been noticed that identifying statements of this sort serve as a preliminary to a description of the object concerned. In the kind of communication which the learners will eventually be dealing with, therefore, the following identification + description sequence is, we will suppose, quite common:

This is a (thermometer). It is used to (measure temperatures).

Now it might also be discovered that the structure 'Here is . . .' is used to express an identification as well, and that the structures: 'It is used for . . . ing . . .' and 'Its use is to . . .' also occur as possible realizations of the act of description. If we grade the language items we have selected for our course in terms of their linguistic complexity, or in such a way that structurally similar items occur together, then 'This is . . .' and 'Here is . . .' and 'Here we have . . .' are likely to occur in different parts of the syllabus, as of course are 'It is used to . . .' and 'It is used for . . . ing . . .' and 'Its use is to . . .' The reason they are placed in different parts of the syllabus is because the grading has operated on the principle of similarity in terms of usage. But if we think in terms of use, then we would wish to arrange these items in such a way as to make it clear that, in the particular kind of communication the course is concerned with (though not necessarily in others), 'This is . . .' 'Here is . . .' 'Here we have . . .' can be grouped together as having the same value as use: they are all used to realize the act of identification. Furthermore, since in this particular kind of communication an identification is commonly followed by a description, the language items introduced after these would logically be not those which resembled them as usage but those which realized that act of description which followed the act of identification. Thus, whereas usage considerations might lead us to separate 'This is . . .' from 'Here is . . .' and both of these from 'It is used to . . .' use considerations would incline us to group the first two together (with perhaps others) and have them followed directly by the second group of structures we have been considering. In this way, the grading itself partially realizes the value these linguistic elements have in this particular kind of communication.

It might be useful at this point to look at the likely results of employing usage criteria and compare them with what might emerge if use criteria were employed instead. The left hand column below shows the sequence of items which is typical of a structurally graded syllabus (that is to say, where usage criteria are employed). The right-hand column shows the sequence which might result from applying use criteria and where the items are grouped together, therefore, in terms of their value in the kind of communication the course is designed to teach.

Grading by reference to usage	Grading by reference to use
This is . . .	This is . . .
That is . . .	Here is . . .
. . . is here.	Here we have . . .
. . . is there	. . . is used for . . .
Here is . . .	. . . is used to . . .
There is . . .	We use . . . to . . .
. . . is + adj	The use of . . . is . . .
This . . . is + adj	. . . is made of . . .

It should be noted that it is not being suggested that all the items in the use grading column should be necessarily taught for productive purposes. If these structures are commonly used to identify and describe in the kind of language use the learners are concerned with, then they will presumably have to learn that they have this common value in order to understand what is being expressed, either in speech or in writing. But for their own productive purposes it would obviously be economical to concentrate on only one of the structures having this common value.

The essential point about grading by reference to use is that the order in which the language items are arranged is intended to reflect their value in the particular kind of communication with which the course is concerned. The sequence that has been given in the right hand column above, for example, can be said to reflect the value that these items take on in passages of use like the following:

This is a hand file. It is used for removing metal from a surface. It is made of hardened steel. etc.

Here we have a hacksaw. The use of a hacksaw is to make thin cuts in metal. Its blade is made of very tough steel. etc.

The value of the items selected for a course, then, can be partially realized by the very manner in which they are ordered in the syllabus by the grading process. The completion of the realization takes place when these language items are presented in the classroom as instances of actual use. As has already been implied, this is no easy task, particularly when the language course is a 'general' one and when, therefore, the ultimate communicative behaviour of the learners has not been clearly defined. As was pointed out at the beginning of this chapter, it is not very satisfactory to speak of the aims of a language course in terms of the ability to speak, understand, write and read the words and structures of a language. We might do better to think instead in terms of the ability to use the language for communicative purposes.[5] But if we think in this way, the potential value of the items we select and their realization as use through grading and presentation have to relate to particular areas of use. What we have to think of, in other words, are particular kinds of communication, particular ways of using the language, as a necessary preliminary to the preparation of the course we are to teach.

A common assumption among language teachers seems to be, as was pointed out earlier, that the essential task is to teach a selection of words and structures, that is to say elements of usage, and that this alone will provide for communicative needs in whichever area of use is relevant to the learner at a more advanced stage. What I am suggesting is that we should think of an area (or areas) of use right from the beginning and base our selection, grading and presentation on that. Only in this way, it seems to me, can we ensure that we are teaching language as communication and not as a stock of usage which may never be realized in actual use at all.

1.6 Selecting areas of use for teaching language

The question now arises: which areas of use would appear to be most suitable for learners at, let us say, the secondary level, the level at which most 'general' foreign language courses are introduced? I should like to suggest that the most likely areas are those of the other subjects on the school curriculum. It is a common view among language teachers that they should attempt to associate the language they are teaching with situations outside the classroom, to what they frequently refer to as 'the real world' of the family, holidays, sports, pastimes and so on. But the school is also part of the child's real world, that part where familiar experience is formalized and extended into new concepts. Subjects like history, geography, general science, art and so on draw upon the reality of the child's own experience and there seems no reason why a foreign language should not relate to the 'outside world' indirectly through them. People who object to making the teaching of a language 'just a school subject' seem to misunderstand what it is that a school subject aims to achieve.

I would argue, then, that a foreign language can be associated with those areas of use which are represented by the other subjects on the school curriculum and that this not only helps to ensure the link with reality and the pupils' own experience but also provides us with the most certain means we have of teaching the language as communication, as use, rather than simply as usage. The kind of language course that I envisage is one which deals with a selection of topics taken from the other subjects: simple experiments in physics and chemistry, biological processes in plants and animals, map-drawing, descriptions of basic geological features, descriptions of historical events and so on. Topics like these should also give ample opportunity for the use of non-linguistic devices in teaching, the importance of which I shall be discussing later on in this book.

It is easy to see that if such a procedure were adopted, the difficulties associated with the presentation of language use in the classroom would, to a considerable degree, disappear. The presentation would essentially be the same as the methodological techniques used for introducing the topics in the subjects from which they are drawn. The presentation of the language used in, for example, a physics experiment would be the same as the presentation of that experiment in the physics laboratory. Now it might be objected that this would mean that the language teacher would have to be familiar with the subjects taught by his colleagues and that this would impose an impossible burden upon him. It is of course true that he would have to familiarize himself with the topics which are included in his syllabus, and with the methodology generally used in teaching them, but the difficulty of this task is easily exaggerated. After all, the language teacher always has to know about something other than the language he is teaching. Traditionally, this knowledge has been of the culture and literature associated with the particular language in question. Thus, the English teacher is expected to know a good deal about British and/or American institutions, social customs, traditions and so on since his textbooks so often draw freely from such sources for their 'subject matter'. A language course has to make use of topic areas of one kind or another if the language is not to be taught as linguistics or philology. All that is being suggested is that the teacher should acquire some limited knowledge of the subjects taught by his colleagues.

One or two other possible advantages of the approach being proposed might be mentioned at this point. First of all, it might persuade the pupil of the immediate relevance of his language learning. The principal difficulty of defining the aims of learning in terms of remote objectives is that they do not provide the pupil with any immediate motivation. If he can be shown, however, that the foreign language can be used to deal with topics which he is concerned with in his other lessons, then he is likely to be aware of its practical relevance as a means of communication. It is true that he does not actually need to learn the foreign language to pursue his studies (at this stage in his education at least) but it will be presented to him not as a body of abstruse and unnecessary knowledge (as is so often the case) but as something which has a definite practical usefulness. One might also make the point that some pupils will actually require the language they are learning to follow further studies in just those areas of enquiry with which it is associated: in many countries, higher education in the physical and social sciences and in different technologies depends heavily on an efficient knowledge of a foreign language. For pupils who will pass on to higher education, the proposed approach would appear to be of particular relevance. But even for those who will not proceed so far in their studies (perhaps the majority) or for those in countries where a foreign language is not required for higher education, the approach will guarantee that learners have had an experience of language as communication, that they have acquired an ability to deal with certain areas of language use which can be extended where necessary into other areas. It is likely to be easier to extend a knowledge of use into new situations and other kinds of discourse than it is to transfer a knowledge of usage, no matter how extensive, to an ability to use this knowledge in the actual business of communication.

The matter of transfer of ability relates to a more general issue in language teaching pedagogy. It seems to me that an over-concentration on usage may often have the effect of putting the language being learned at a remove from the learner's own experience of language. As I indicated earlier, normal communication operates at the level of use and we are not generally aware of the usage aspect of performance. By focussing on usage, therefore, the language teacher directs the attention of the learner to those features of performance which normal use of language requires him to ignore. Thus, the way the foreign language is presented in the classroom does not correspond with the learner's experience of his own language outside the classroom, or in the classrooms where he uses the language in his study of other subjects. On the contrary, the way he is required to learn the foreign language conflicts with the way he knows language actually works, and this necessarily impedes any transfer which might otherwise take place. By effectively denying the learner reference to his own experience the teacher increases the difficulty of the language learning task. A methodology which concentrates too exclusively on usage may well be creating the very problems which it is designed to solve.

Another advantage I would wish to claim for the subject-oriented approach I have suggested relates to this point about transfer from the learner's own experience. It is this: since the topics dealt with in the language course will also be dealt with in other lessons through the medium of the mother tongue, then the pupils can make use of translation in their learning of the foreign language. This is a controversial matter because many teachers would regard it as a disadvantage. They would say that the use of the mother tongue distracts the learner's attention from the ways in which the foreign language expresses meaning. I think that this may indeed be true when the translation involves relating two languages word for word or sentence for sentence: that is to say, where the translation operates at the level of usage. But in the case of the approach that is being proposed, translation would not operate at this level but at the level of use. That is to say, the learner would recognize that acts of communication, like identification, description, instruction and so on, are expressed in the foreign language in one way and in his own language in another. He would, therefore, equate two sentences only with reference to their use in communication and this should help to impress upon him the values that the foreign language sentences can assume, which is precisely the aim we wish to achieve.

1.7   Summary and conclusion

Let me now summarize the main points that have been made in this chapter. I have suggested that a distinction might be made between language usage and language use. The first of these is the citation of words and sentences as manifestations of the language system, and the second is the way the system is realized for normal communicative purposes. Knowing a language is often taken to mean having a knowledge of correct usage but this knowledge is of little utility on its own: it has to be complemented by a knowledge of appropriate use. A knowledge of use must of necessity include a knowledge of usage but the reverse is not the case: it is possible for someone to have learned a large number of sentence patterns and a large number of words which can fit into them without knowing how they are actually put to communicative use.

Both the manifestation of the language system as usage and its realization as use have meaning but the meaning is of a different kind in each case. Words and sentences have meaning because they are part of a language system and this meaning is recorded in grammars and dictionaries. The term signification was used to refer to this kind of meaning: the meaning that sentences have in isolation from a linguistic context or from a particular situation in which the sentence is produced. This was distinguished from what was called value, and this was defined as the meaning that sentences take on when they are put to use in order to perform different acts of communication. Thus the signification of the following sentence:

The policeman is crossing the road

can be found by recognizing that here we have a declarative sentence (as opposed to an interrogative one), that the verb is present in tense (as opposed to past) and continuous in aspect (as opposed to perfective or 'unmarked') and so on: the signification is derived from the relationship between the grammatical meanings of the syntactic choices and the dictionary meanings of the lexical items *policeman*, *cross* and *road*. In terms of value, however, this sentence might serve a number of different communicative functions depending on the contextual and/or situational circumstances in which it were used. Thus, it might take on the value of part of a commentary (our man in the telephone box), or it might serve as a warning or a threat, or some other act of communication.

If it is the case that knowing a language means both knowing what signification sentences have as instances of usage and what value they take on as instances of use, it seems clear that the teacher of language should be concerned with the teaching of both kinds of knowledge. In the past the tendency has been to concentrate on usage on the assumption that learners will eventually pick up the necessary knowledge of use on their own. This would seem to be too optimistic a view to take. The evidence seems to be that learners who have acquired a good deal of knowledge of the usage of a particular language find themselves at a loss when they are confronted with actual instances of use. The teaching of usage does not appear to guarantee a knowledge of use. The teaching of use, however, does seem to guarantee the learning of usage since the latter is represented as a necessary part of the former. This being so, it would seem to be sensible to design language teaching courses with reference to use. This does not mean that exercises in particular aspects of usage cannot be introduced where necessary; but these would be auxiliary to the communicative purposes of the course as a whole and not introduced as an end in themselves.

It was suggested that perhaps the best way of doing this was to associate the teaching of a foreign language with topics drawn from other subjects on the school curriculum. It might be added here that even if there are administrative and other difficulties in the way of adopting such an approach from the beginning, it should be possible to do so at a later stage of learning. I think that it is possible, in principle, to teach use in the way that it has been proposed from the first language lesson, but particular practical factors may not be favourable for applying this principle. What is important is not that the teacher should embrace this suggestion as an absolute dogma to be adhered to unthinkingly, but that he should consider its possibilities and put it into practice at what seems to be the most appropriate and practicable time.

In the discussion of use earlier in this chapter, it was pointed out that a sentence might be appropriate in a particular context by virtue of its form but still not be appropriate in function in a particular situation. The notion of appropriacy, then, was applied both to the form and the function of sentences as instances of use. The nature of the relationship between formal and functional appropriacy will be discussed in more detail in the chapter which follows.

Notes and references

1. For accounts of these distinctions and their relevance to language teaching see:

   J. P. B. Allen: 'Some basic concepts in linguistics' in *The Edinburgh Course in Applied Linguistics* (henceforth ECAL) *Volume 2:* Edited by J. P. B. Allen & S. Pit Corder, Oxford University Press, 1975, pp. 37–40.
   D. A. Wilkins: *Linguistics in Language Teaching*, Arnold, 1972, pp. 33–6.

2. I do not wish to suggest that signification and value are quite distinct and unrelated aspects of meaning. Obviously they are not. The value which a word or sentence assumes when put to communicative use must in part depend on signification since communication can only take place by reference to a shared system of signs, a shared code. Value is the function of the relationship between code and context. Signification is a necessary but not a sufficient condition for communication to take place.

3. Situations of this sort are ingeniously introduced into the Penguin English Course *Success with English*.
   See in particular Geoffrey Broughton: Coursebook 1, Unit 1.

4. The most detailed treatment is to be found in W. F. Mackey: *Language Teaching Analysis*, Longman, 1965, pp. 137 et seq. The criteria discussed by Mackey are: frequency, range, availability, coverage, learnability. See also Chapters 29–31 of my *Language Teaching Texts*, Oxford University Press, 1971 and my paper 'The teaching of English through Science' in Julian Dakin, Brian Tiffen and H. G. Widdowson: *Language in Education*, Oxford University Press, 1968.

5. For a detailed discussion of the advantages of adopting a communicative orientation to syllabus design see D. A. Wilkins: *Notional Syllabuses*, Oxford University Press, 1976.

2 Discourse

2.1 Sentence, proposition and illocutionary act

The discussion in the preceding chapter makes it clear that although we can consider usage by restricting our attention to sentences, the consideration of use requires us to go beyond the sentence and to look at larger stretches of language. Normal linguistic behaviour does not consist in the production of separate sentences but in the use of sentences for the creation of *discourse*. In this chapter I want to enquire into how the notion of discourse might be characterized.

We may begin by pointing out that when people produce a sentence in the course of normal communicative activity they simultaneously do two things. They express a proposition of one kind or another and at the same time in expressing that proposition they perform some kind of illocutionary act.[1] To illustrate this, let us imagine that during a conversation between two people one of them (A) makes the following remark:

A: My husband will return the parcel tomorrow.

Now if the other person taking part in the conversation (B) wishes to report this remark to a third person, he can do so in one of three ways. He may make use of direct speech:

B: She said: 'My husband will return the parcel tomorrow.'

Here B is reporting A's *sentence*. Alternatively, he can use indirect speech:

B: She said that her husband would return the parcel tomorrow.

In this case it is not A's sentence that is being reported but the *proposition* that her sentence is used to express. Now whereas there is only one possible version of A's remark as a sentence, there are several possible versions of her remark taken as the expression of a proposition. Thus all of the following represent accurate reports:

B: (i) She said that the parcel would be returned by her husband tomorrow.

(ii) She said that it would be her husband who would return the parcel tomorrow.

(iii) She said that it would be the parcel that her husband would return tomorrow.

(iv) She said that what her husband would do tomorrow would be to return the parcel.

and so on.

I will return presently to the question of what controls the choice of one version rather than another. But first let us note the third way in which B can report A's remark. This involves him in specifying what *illocutionary act* he supposed A was performing at the time. Depending on the circumstances of utterance, what has preceded in the conversation, what B knows of the situation, the relationship between A and her husband, between A, B and the person that B is reporting to, the nature of the parcel, and so on, B might interpret A's remark in a number of ways, and report it accordingly. The following, then, are all possible:

B: She promised that her husband would return the parcel tomorrow.
She threatened that her husband would return the parcel tomorrow.
She warned me that her husband would return the parcel tomorrow.
She predicted that her husband would return the parcel tomorrow.
She mentioned in passing that her husband would return the parcel tomorrow.

Notice that in reporting these acts (promise, threat, warning, prediction, casual comment) B at the same time reports A's proposition, but not her sentence. Thus he can use any of the versions given earlier:

B: She promised that the parcel would be returned by her husband tomorrow.
She warned me that it would be her husband who would return the parcel tomorrow.
and so on.

The following, however, are not normally possible:

B: She promised: 'My husband will return the parcel tomorrow.'
She warned: 'My husband will return the parcel tomorrow.'

We can now take up the question of what it is that determines B's choice of a particular version. Each version represents a different way of organizing the information expressed in the proposition. If B decides that the person he is reporting to (C) is principally interested in the parcel rather than the husband, then he will be inclined to use version (i). If, on the other hand, he thinks that C might be in some doubt as to what it is that the husband is to return, then he might be inclined to stress the fact that it is the parcel (and not, say, the money or something else) that is to be returned and he would accordingly select version (iii). If he feels that C might be uncertain whether it is the husband or somebody else who is to do the returning of the parcel, then he would be likely to prefer version (ii). B's decision, then, is dependent on what he knows of C's state of knowledge, on what he judges C needs to be informed about. Now B may be familiar with C's state of knowledge beforehand: it may be part of the situation. Thus B may meet C after having talked to A and the following exchange may ensue:

C: Well?
B: She said that the parcel would be returned by her husband tomorrow.

Here B is already aware that C knows about the parcel and that C wants to know what is going to happen to it. It may indeed be the case that the parcel is of such over-riding importance to the two of them that no specific reference to it need be made at all. We might have this exchange:

C: Well?
B: She said that it would be returned by her husband tomorrow.

Again, it might be that both B and C already know that the parcel is to be returned and that A's husband is to do the returning, but that they do not know when. In this case, B's reply could take the following form:

C: Well?
B: She said it would be tomorrow that her husband would return the parcel.

Or, again, B might judge that such explicitness is unnecessary on the grounds that both he and C already know about the parcel and the husband. In this case, we might simply get:

C: Well?
B: Tomorrow.

2.2 Cohesion and propositional development

In all of these examples, B makes a decision about which sentence or part of a sentence is needed based on his previous familiarity with C's state of knowledge and his interest, with what C needs to know or wants to know. This previous familiarity is part of the situation. But this state of knowledge or interest might also emerge in conversation and therefore control the form of the propositions that C himself expresses. In this case, the sentences, or parts of sentences, uttered by both B and C would be such as to ensure that each proposition fitted in with the others. This is what was meant in Chapter 1 when I referred to sentences which were contextually appropriate. Sentences are contextually appropriate when they express propositions in such a way as to fit into the propositional development of the discourse as a whole. Consider, for example, the following exchange:

C: Well, did you talk to her?
B: Yes, I did (talk to her).
C: When did she say the parcel would be returned?
B: (She said that the parcel would be returned) tomorrow.
C: Good. I'll meet her at the shop.
B: She said that her husband would return it.

Here C's questions take on a form which indicates what he needs to know and B's replies organize the information he has to impart in such a way as to satisfy C's need. Thus the propositions expressed by C are linked up with those expressed by B to form a continuous propositional development. We can say that the forms of the utterances of B and C are contextually appropriate and so ensure that their exchange is *cohesive*.

Referring back to Chapter 1, we can now explain why the exchanges cited at the beginning of the chapter represent odd combinations of sentences:

A: What did the rain do?
B: The crops were destroyed by the rain.

A's question makes it clear that what he does not know is what the rain did but he knows that the rain did something. Generally speaking we can say that propositions are organized in such a way that what is known, or given, comes first in the sentence, and what is unknown or new, comes second. But here B's sentence arranges the propositional information in such a way as to suggest that A already knows about the crops, whereas it is precisely this information he is asking for. These two sentences do not, therefore, combine to form a cohesive unit. To achieve cohesion we have to alter the form either of A's sentences or of B's:

A: What happened to the crops?
B: The crops were destroyed by the rain.
They were destroyed by the rain.
Destroyed by the rain.

Note that it is because the information about the crops is given that B's reply does not need to make specific reference to them: the pronoun *they* takes on the value in this context of the full reference *the crops*. And, indeed, as the third version of B's response makes clear, there need be no reference to the topic of discussion at all: B can produce part of a sentence only and this will take on the value of the complete proposition by its relationship with the proposition expressed through A's sentence. The same points can be made about the result of altering the form of B's response:

A: What did the rain do?
B: The rain destroyed the crops.
   It destroyed the crops.
   Destroyed the crops.

The notion of cohesion, then, refers to the way sentences and parts of sentences combine so as to ensure that there is propositional development. Usually sentences used communicatively in discourse do not in themselves express independent propositions: they take on value in relation to other propositions expressed through other sentences. If we can recognize this relationship and so are able to associate a sentence, or part of a sentence, with an appropriate value, then we recognize a sequence of sentences or sentence-parts as constituting cohesive discourse. The difficulty we have in recovering propositional development is a measure of the degree of cohesion exhibited by a particular discourse. The difficulty might arise because the form of a sentence represents an inappropriate arrangement of information in respect to what has preceded: the work we have to do in making the necessary readjustment disturbs the propositional development, and to this extent impairs effective communication. Similarly, unnecessary repetition of what is already known, or given, may reduce communicative effectiveness because the important, unknown, parts of the proposition tend to become over-shadowed by what is known: they are not brought into prominence. Consider, for example, the following:

A: What happened to the crops?
B: The crops were destroyed by the rain.
A: When were the crops destroyed by the rain?
B: The crops were destroyed by the rain last week.

This is not a normal instance of use because each sentence represents an independent expression of the proposition. We need to fuse them together by removing redundancies so that propositional development is carried forward. The following is cohesive in a way that the above exchange of sentences is not:

A: What happened to the crops?
B: They were destroyed by the rain.
A: When?
B: Last week.

We may say that a discourse is cohesive to the extent that it allows for effective propositional development and we may say that sentences are appropriate in form to the extent that they allow for this development. Further, this appropriacy will often require sentences *not* to express complete propositions.

2.3 Coherence and illocutionary development

Now in the cases we have just been considering, cohesion is a matter of the contextual appropriacy of linguistic forms—sentences and parts of sentences. We can recognize propositional links because of our knowledge of certain facts about the English language. Thus we know that a pronoun like *it* functions anaphorically: that is to say, it copies certain features of a previous noun (+singular, −human) and so serves to repeat the reference in an economical and unobtrusive way. We know that *do* is a pro-verb which functions in a similar fashion for a previous verbal reference. We know that when we are confronted with an incomplete sentence like *destroyed by rain*, there must be some linguistic item previously given which can serve as subject to complete the sentence. In other words, the cohesion we have been considering can be described in terms of the formal (syntactic and semantic) links between sentences and their parts. The cohesion is overtly signalled.[2]

But discourse is not dependent on overt cohesion of this kind. Although propositional development can be overtly signalled in this way, it is common to find instances of discourse which appear not to be cohesive at all. It is at this point that we must turn our attention to illocutionary acts. As the preceding discussion has made clear, language use does not just mean the production of sentences in sequence but the expression of propositions through sentences. But as was pointed out in the early part of this chapter, when we use language we do not just express propositions either: we perform illocutionary acts of one kind or another in the expressing of propositions. The description of discourse involves in part accounting for the way propositions combine to form an ongoing development: but it also involves accounting for the illocutionary acts these propositions are used to perform, and how they are related to each other.

We might compare the following exchanges:

1. A: What are the police doing?
   B: They are arresting the demonstrators.

2. A: What are the police doing?
   B: The fascists are arresting the demonstrators.

3. A: What are the police doing?
   B: I have just arrived.

In the first of these examples, the anaphoric item *they* signals a propositional link with the preceding sentence and we can provide the full reference *the police* without difficulty. The cohesion in 2 is rather more difficult to arrive at (and so we might say that it is less cohesive). The definite noun phrase signals that there is a reference to something previously mentioned, or to something which can be pointed to the immediate situation of utterance (that is to say, it is either anaphoric or deictic). If we assume that B is referring to something that A has said, and that his remark is intended as a response, then we must assume the definite noun phrase to be anaphoric. This assumption allows us to establish a semantic link between *the police* and *the fascists*. If we know that for certain groups of people these two terms are often associated (sometimes to the extent of being virtually synonymous), then this eases our task of linking the propositions and the exchange is correspondingly more cohesive.

In the case of 1 and 2, there are formal signals which enable us to recover the propositional link between the two remarks. But in 3 there are no such formal signals. Whereas in 1 and 2 there were connections across sentences, there are no connections whatever between the sentence uttered by A and that uttered by B in 3. In spite of this, it is not difficult to recognize that B's remark could be an entirely appropriate one. Why is this so?

The answer is that we make sense of 3 by focussing our attention on the illocutionary acts which the propositions are being used to perform. We create a situation in our minds which will provide us with an illocutionary link between the two utterances. We might envisage a situation, for example, in which there is some kind of disturbance involving the police which attracts the attention of passers-by. A crowd gathers, and one bystander (A) asks another (B) what is going on. B's remark can now be interpreted as an explanation for his inability to answer A's question: he cannot provide the information requested because he has just appeared on the scene. Now once we recognize what the proposition expressed by B counts as in this situation as an illocutionary act, we can supply the missing propositional link in the following way:

A: What are the police doing?
B: (I don't know what the police are doing because) I have just arrived.

I want to suggest that where we can establish a propositional relationship across sentences, without regard to what illocutionary acts are being performed, by reference to formal syntactic and semantic signals, then we recognize *cohesion*. Cohesion, then, is the overt relationship between propositions expressed through sentences. Where we recognize that there is a relationship between the illocutionary acts which propositions, not always overtly linked, are being used to perform, then we are perceiving the *coherence* of the discourse. In these terms, of the exchanges given above, 1 and 2 are cohesive and coherent and 3 is coherent without being cohesive. In the case of cohesion, we can infer the illocutionary acts from the propositional connections which are overtly indicated: in the case of coherence we infer the covert propositional connections from an interpretation of the illocutionary acts.

Let me try and clarify this distinction between the propositional and illocutionary features of discourse by considering another example. It is not difficult to provide the following interchange with a plausible interpretation, in spite of the complete absence of cohesion:

A: That's the telephone.
B: I'm in the bath.
A: O.K.

How do we make sense of this? That is to say, how do we recognize this as a coherent instance of discourse?[3] What we do, of course, is to envisage a situation in which the uttering of the first of these sentences (A's first remark) would be understood as constituting a request. Notice that it is not an interrogative sentence but a declarative sentence that is used. Notice, too, that in isolation the proposition expressed by this sentence cannot take on any particular communicative value: and in other situations it might count as a number of other acts—an identification, a warning, an explanation and so on. The reason we give it the value of a request in this case is that we recognize the way in which it relates to the other parts of the exchange here. Taken together, we recognize B's remark as a reply to A's and as having the communicative value of an excuse for not complying with A's request, and we recognize A's second remark as an acceptance of B's excuse and as an undertaking to do himself (or herself) what he (she) originally asked B to do. Once one establishes a relationship between the three utterances as illocutionary acts and thereby sees them as constituting a coherent discourse, one can then supply the missing propositional links and produce a version which *is* cohesive:

A: That's the telephone. (Can you answer it, please?)
B: (No, I can't answer it because) I'm in the bath.
A: O.K. (I'll answer it).

2.4 The relationship between propositional and illocutionary development

The notions of cohesion and coherence have so far been illustrated by reference only to spoken discourse, and spoken discourse, what is more,

of an overtly interactive kind: all the examples have been of conversational exchanges. But the points that have been raised apply also
to written discourse, and in general to other forms of spoken discourse
(like speeches, lectures) which involve only one speaker. In all kinds
of discourse one can trace propositional development through cohesion
and illocutionary development through coherence, and all discourse
can be characterized in terms of the relationship between propositions
and illocutionary acts.

To illustrate this point, let us consider the following:

The committee decided to continue with its arrangements.
Morgan left London on the midnight train.

Presented in this way, on separate lines, these are simply instances of
usage: two isolated sentences manifesting certain rules of the system of
English. But if we present them as a sequence, then we have to consider
them as use:

The committee decided to continue with its arrangements. Morgan left
London on the midnight train.

Since they are now presented as discourse, our task is to realize those
relationships between the propositions and acts expressed by these
sentences that make them into a discourse. How do we proceed?

There are no linguistic signals of a syntactic or semantic kind which
will enable us to establish any cohesive links between the propositions
expressed in these two sentences. All we can do, therefore, is to make
sense of them by providing them with an illocutionary value. There are a
number of possibilities here. We might, for example, interpret the second
proposition as having the value of a qualifying statement of some kind
which in some sense 'corrects' what is stated in the first proposition. We
can make this interpretation explicit by using what we will call an
illocutionary marker: *however*.

The committee decided to continue with its arrangements. Morgan,
however, left London on the midnight train.

Once we have attributed a certain illocutionary value to the second proposition, we are in a position to see what inferences are required to fill
the gap between the second proposition and the first. We infer, for
example, that the committee's arrangements should have prevented
Morgan's departure. To make the discourse cohesive we could write in
something to that effect:

The committee decided to continue with its arrangements. (These
arrangements required Morgan to remain in London.) Morgan, however, left London on the midnight train.

Other interpretations are, of course, possible. Morgan can be understood to have acted in accordance with and not in defiance of the committee's arrangements. In this case, the second proposition takes on the value of a logical conclusion, and the two propositions can be seen as realizing a cause/effect relationship. We can make this interpretation explicit by use of the marker *therefore*:

The committee decided to continue with its arrangements. Morgan, therefore, left London on the midnight train.

If we assume this interpretation, then cohesion will be supplied by inferring a different proposition; perhaps something like:

The committee decided to continue with its arrangements. (These arrangements required Morgan to leave London.) Morgan, therefore, left London on the midnight train.

Other interpretations are possible, but perhaps enough has been said to indicate that the recovery of the propositional link here crucially depends on the illocutionary value that is given to the two propositions. Now, of course, one does not normally encounter discourses consisting of just two sentences and in this respect this example is a distortion of natural language use. The sentences would normally occur in a linguistic context or an extra-linguistic situation which would provide evidence for how they were to be interpreted. But it is important to note that the context or the situation does not of itself indicate the value that sentences assume in discourse as expressions of propositions and performances of illocutionary acts. This value is inferred by the language user by reference to the evidence at his disposal.

2.5   Procedures of interpretation

I have spoken of cohesion as the overt, linguistically-signalled relationship between propositions and coherence as the relationship between illocutionary acts. These relationships are, it should be noted, discovered by the reader or the listener as a result of rational procedures. Meanings do not exist, ready-made, in the language itself: they are worked out. We are given linguistic clues to what propositions are expressed and what illocutionary acts are performed, and on the basis of these clues we make sense of the sentences. What we do when we produce discourse is to provide as many clues as we think necessary for the satisfactory conveyance of our meanings: we do not express everything we mean. Indeed, it is probably impossible to do this even if it were necessary. But it is not necessary. We inevitably rely on common knowledge: we make assumptions about what the person we are addressing can infer from what we say. If we judge correctly and make the right assumptions, then the person being addressed will be able to reconstitute our meanings on the basis of the clues we provide and with reference to the knowledge he shares with us. Of course, this does not necessarily mean that what the discourse producer creates will be the same as what the discourse receiver re-creates. Apart from the fact that the latter may miss or misinterpret certain clues, his purpose in processing the discourse may not require him to recover all the meaning that the producer intends. These points have relevance for the definition of the language skills, which I shall consider in the next chapter.

Meanwhile, the point to be stressed here is that the use of language in discourse is an essentially creative endeavour which involves the language user in working out propositional and illocutionary development. It may be, as in the case of Morgan and the committee, that the realization of communicative value will reveal what is implied or presupposed but not made explicit by cohesive links. It may be that in interpreting a particular discourse we are led to infer the illocutionary value of propositions and their coherent relationship by first recognizing the cohesive links that obtain between them. In either case, the discourse is interpreted by our understanding how sentences are used for propositional and illocutionary development and how these two aspects of discourse inter-relate and reinforce each other.

2.6   Deriving discourse from sentences: an example

Discourse is, of course, also *produced* by reference to the same understanding. The speaker (or writer) provides as many clues to his intended meanings as he judges to be necessary for the listener (or reader) he is addressing to recover them, relying on knowledge of the world, of the conventions of the language code and of the convention of use which he assumes to be shared. To illustrate the points that I have been making in this chapter, therefore, we might begin with a set of sentences and consider what is involved in creating a discourse out of them. As we proceed, we shall be led towards a further refinement of the notions we have been considering. Here are the sentences:

1. Rocks are composed of a number of different substances.
2. The different substances of which rocks are composed are called minerals.
3. It is according to their chemical composition that minerals are classified.
4. Some minerals are oxides.
5. Some minerals are sulphides.
6. Some minerals are silicates.
7. Ores are minerals from which we extract metals.
8. What gold is is an ore.

Presented in this way, as a list, each sentence is an isolated unit expressing a self-contained proposition. Confronted with a list of this sort, we would not normally trouble to look for any relationship between the items. If we were to present them end to end, however, they would immediately take on the appearance of an instance of written discourse:

Rocks are composed of a number of different substances. The different substances of which rocks are composed are called minerals. It is according to their chemical composition that minerals are classified. Some minerals are oxides. etc.

Our interpretative strategies are now engaged and we seek to establish relations between the sentences which will yield a satisfactory propositional and illocutionary development. Once these relations are established, we can restructure the individual sentences so as to realize them. That is to say, we can *textualize* our understanding of these sentences as components of a discourse, thereby providing them with a unifying cohesion and coherence.

2.6.1 *Propositional development: achieving cohesion*

We will begin with the second sentence (S2). This clearly presupposes the first (S1): the phrase 'the different substances of which rocks are composed' simply repeats the information given in S1 and so is redundant. At the same time, there must be some means whereby the proposition in S1 is linked to the proposition in S2: there needs to be a referential reminder of some kind, a so-called anaphoric element which recalls something previously mentioned. Thus the writer will use a linguistic element which copies those semantic features of previous reference which he judges to be necessary to remind the reader of what has been said before. In the present case, what would seem to be needed is an anaphoric element which copies the feature of plurality. In English we have two possibilities: 'they' and 'these'. Which one are we to choose?

Let us first notice that in the first sentence there are two noun phrases in the plural: 'rocks' and 'different substances' and so it would follow that a reminder which simply copied plurality would be ambiguous: it would not be as effective a clue as it might be. But as it happens, one of these pronouns carries a feature other than that which simply indicates plurality. It is commonly the case that when there are two previous references to which these pronouns could refer, 'these' is used if it is the second which is to be carried over into the following proposition. 'These', we might say, has the additional implicational feature of closer proximity and could be glossed as meaning 'these last mentioned', or 'the latter'. Thus, to add a little variety to our examples, if we were asked to complete the second of the following sentences:

The generals decided that it was time to put their plans into operation. They . . .

we would be inclined to say something about the generals and not about their plans. If, on the other hand, we were to be presented with the following:

The generals decided that it was time to put their plans into operation. These . . .

then the likelihood is that we would want to say something about the plans rather than about the generals. If we wished to guard against any possible misunderstanding, therefore, we would rewrite S2 as:

These are called minerals.

We may, of course, feel that even this does not make a sufficiently explicit link with S1. In this case, we could copy more of the previous reference:

These substances are called minerals.

There are, then, a number of ways in which we can make S2 dependent on S1 so as to establish a cohesive link between them. Which way we choose will depend on our judgement about the capacity of the reader to recover the relationship between the propositions expressed. We might, after all, decide that the redundancy in S2 should be retained for the particular readers we have in mind. On the other hand, we might decide that S2 can be suppressed altogether by making an adjustment to S3, to which sentence we now turn.

Whereas in S2 we were concerned with appropriate reduction of redundancy and the establishing of a minimally adequate referential reminder, in S3 we are concerned with the arrangement of the sentence constituents. Generally speaking, as was pointed out earlier in this chapter, we may say that in English what comes first in the sentence expresses information which is assumed to be known, or given, and what comes afterwards expresses information which is assumed to be new. Thus, to recall our previous example, the use of the following sentence:

The crops were destroyed by rain

presupposes that the topic 'crops' has already been broached in conversation or is in some other way understood to be the matter at issue. The speaker assumes that the person he is addressing knows about the crops but does not know what happened to them. So the sentence cited here would serve as an appropriate response to a question like:

What happened to the crops?

But it would not be an appropriate response to a question of the form:

What did the rain do?

because here the topic 'rain' is given by the question, which accordingly requires a response which presents this information at the beginning of the sentence:

The rain destroyed the crops.

Now in the case of S3, the topic 'minerals' has already been introduced in S2 and is therefore given. Its appropriate place in S3 is, in consequence, at the beginning of the sentence:

Minerals are classified according to their chemical composition.

This seems simple enough, but it will be interesting to enquire what is presupposed in terms of given and new by S3 as originally presented.

Let us start by considering the following:

It was the rain that destroyed the crops.

As with S3, what we have here is a so-called 'cleft' sentence. The effect of such sentences is to separate out what is given information and place it, parenthetically so to speak, within the subordinate clause. The new information then appears in prominent and contrastive position at the end of the main clause. Thus, in our sentence about the rain and the crops, the assumption is that it is already known that something destroyed the crops and the speaker wishes to stress that it was the rain, and not, say, the snow or the ice, that destroyed them. The use of sentences of this kind, then, presents new information in a particularly forceful way in order to correct what the speaker believes to be a wrong assumption. Put another way, it serves to superimpose new information on information already given but incorrect. We might compare the following:

The rain destroyed the crops (given: the rain did something)
The crops were destroyed by the rain (given: the crops were destroyed)
It was the rain that destroyed the crops (given: the (e.g.) snow destroyed the crops)
It was the crops that were destroyed by the rain (given: the (e.g.) flowers were destroyed by the rain)

Now with regard to S3; its form presupposes that the question as to how minerals are classified has already been touched on whereas the preceding sentences have not mentioned the matter: the issue of classification is new. It further presupposes that some other means of classification has been proposed other than chemical composition since the phrase 'according to their chemical composition' is placed in prominent and contrastive position as new information. We can textualize these presuppositions by rewriting S3 as follows:

As far as classification is concerned, it is according to their chemical composition and not according to their colour or shape that minerals are classified.

Once the presuppositions of S3 are written out in this way, its inappropriacy in this context becomes clear.

In order to have S3 continue the propositional development from S1 and S2, then, we need to re-organize the constituents to produce something like:

Minerals are classified according to their chemical composition.

We might, of course, (bearing in mind our discussion of S1 and S2) consider that the repetition of the term 'minerals' is unnecessary and choose to replace it with an anaphoric element which simply copies the feature of plurality:

They are classified according to their chemical composition.

Alternatively, as was suggested earlier, we might place more reliance on the reader's ability to infer meanings by leaving S2 out altogether and adjusting S3 to read:

These minerals are classified according to their chemical composition.

Here, the use of the demonstrative adjective 'these' serves as a directive to the reader to relate the term 'minerals' to something previously mentioned, which in this case can only be the substances of which rocks are composed referred to in S1. The reader can thus infer that these substances are called minerals without having this explicitly stated in a sentence such as S2.

We now turn to S4, S5 and S6. These can be dealt with quite briefly. Each of them exhibits needless repetition of the given information and we can reduce this redundancy by replacing the lexical item 'minerals' with an appropriate anaphoric pronoun. Such a procedure will yield:

Some of them are oxides.
etc.

Or, more succinctly:

Some are oxides.
etc.

It seems a little cumbersome to leave these three sentences as separate entities, and we might feel inclined to combine them into one sentence:

Some are oxides, some are sulphides, some are silicates.

This brings up the question of the criteria for combining sentences which we have not yet discussed, but which we will discuss presently. Meanwhile we have still to deal with S7 and S8.

The use of S7 as it stands would imply, as we have already noted in connection with S3, that the topic 'ores' has already been introduced since it appears in the 'given' position at the beginning of the sentence. Since it is, in fact, new information, this is not appropriate. If we re-organize the sentence so that it does represent an appropriate arrangement of information we get:

Minerals from which we extract metals are ores.

There is something about this sentence, however, that is not entirely satisfactory. One might, indeed, suspect that it is not quite grammatical. Noting its resemblance to S2, we can emend it so that it appears as:

Minerals from which we extract metals are *called* ores.

The question is: why is such an emendation necessary? In our previous re-arrangement operations we have managed to produce quite un-objectionable sentences as more appropriate variants but on this occasion it seems that we have to introduce additional lexical material. To explain why this should be so, we have to move on from a consideration of how information is to be re-organized to ensure propositional development to a consideration of the illocutionary function of these sentences in the discourse we are creating. I will come to that in a moment. For the present we have still to deal with S8.

S8 is an example of a so-called 'pseudo-cleft' sentence. Sentences like this resemble cleft sentences in that they single out items of information for special attention, and function as statements which in some sense correct a previous supposition. To illustrate this, let us return once more to the rain and the crops. The following are pseudo-cleft versions of the sentence:

What the rain did was to destroy the crops.
What happened to the crops was that they were destroyed by the rain.

In the first of these sentences, 'what the rain did' is given and 'destroy the crops' is new. To use this sentence is to assume that it is *known* that the rain did something and it is *thought* that what it did was something other than destroy the crops. In the second sentence, similarly, the first clause 'what happened to the crops' is represented as giving information and the second, 'that they were destroyed by the rain' is represented as new and in some sense corrective of a previous assumption. We can show this information, as before, in roughly the following way:

What the rain did was to destroy the crops (given: the rain did something other than destroy the crops)
What happened to the crops was that they were destroyed by the rain
(given: something else happened to the crops)

Turning now to S8, we can see that what is presupposed here is that a
previous assumption has been made that gold is something other than
an ore. But there is, of course, no evidence for this assumption in the
preceding sentences. We therefore need to emend S8 in some way. The
most obvious way might appear to be to 'de-cleft' and produce:

Gold is an ore.

This seems to follow on quite naturally from what has gone before.
But we have been working on the principle that given information
precedes new information in a sentence and in the present case it is in
fact the topic of 'ore' that has already been introduced, and so should
be represented as given, whereas 'gold' introduces a new topic. Why
then is it that our revised S8 seems to be acceptable? This again is a
question which has to do with the illocutionary development of the
discourse.

Before considering illocutionary development, let us first see the total
effect of the changes we have been making to the original set of
sentences:

Discourse A Rocks are composed of a number of different substances.
These are called minerals. Minerals are classified according to their
chemical composition. Some are oxides. Some are sulphides. Some are
silicates. Minerals from which we extract metals are called ores. Gold
is an ore.

It will perhaps be acknowledged that we have achieved a degree of
cohesion here in that the sentence forms allow for propositional
development. But this is not, of course, the only possible version. So
far, for example, we have retained the same number of sentences as in
the original set. As was indicated in our discussion of S3 and S4-6,
there might be good reasons for combining some of the sentences.
What are these reasons? What criteria do we use for combination?

2.6.2 *Illocutionary development: achieving coherence*

Generally speaking we may say that if a piece of information is incorporated into a separate sentence then it is intended to be taken as having
independent significance. If, for example, two events are described in
two different sentences, then each event is represented as being
significant, in some sense, in its own right. To illustrate this, we might
cite the following:

Morgan left home at midnight. He missed the train.

Here Morgan's leaving home and his missing of the train are represented as two events. Now, as before, if we treat these two sentences as components of a discourse, then our interpretative faculty is activated and we begin to infer a relationship between the events described: we try to create a coherent discourse. We might suppose, for example, that Morgan missed the train because his departure from home at midnight did not leave him enough time to catch it. On the other hand, we might suppose that he missed the train in spite of the fact that he left home with plenty of time in hand. We could, then, understand these two sentences as being related in either of the following ways:

Morgan left home at midnight. He therefore missed the train.
Morgan left home at midnight. Nevertheless he missed the train.

The two events, though now explicitly related, remain distinct, however, each having equal prominence. But if we combine the two sentences, the two events are bound together in some way. We could combine them by co-ordination.:

Morgan left home at midnight and (he) missed the train.

Here the conjunction 'and' functions as an indicator that the two events are meant to be associated: Morgan's leaving home and his missing the train are represented as one item of information. The actual relationship between the events, however, is left unspecified. If we combine the sentences by sub-ordination, on the other hand, this relationship has to be made explicit and one event, that which is referred to in the main clause, takes precedence over the other, that which is referred to in the subsidiary clause:

Morgan missed the train because he left home at midnight.
Although Morgan left home at midnight, he missed the train.

In these cases, the information contained in the subsidiary clause plays a supporting role to that contained in the main clause: it loses its independent status.

We might note, in passing, that the two complex sentences just cited are more likely (and to that extent more acceptable) than the following:

Because Morgan left home at midnight he missed the train.
Morgan missed the train although he left home at midnight.

We can account for the relative unlikelihood of these two sentences by invoking once more the generalization that what appears at the beginning of a sentence is given and what appears at the end is new. Since the *because*-clause provides a reason for an event or a state of affairs one would normally expect that event or state of affairs to be already known and in need of some kind of explanation. Hence it is natural for such a clause to occur as new information following the main clause. The *although*-clause, on the other hand, concedes an item of information (as indeed the traditional grammatical term 'clause of concession' indicates) and this presupposes that what is to be conceded is already known. Hence it is natural for a clause of this 'concessive' kind to occur in the position normally associated with given information and so to appear before the main clause.

To return now to the main theme, the point to be noted is that when sentences are combined by subordination the proposition expressed in one necessarily becomes dependent on the proposition expressed in the other: one becomes prominent at the expense of the other. If we consider our set of rewritten sentences, it will be seen that S1 can be combined with S2 in a number of ways. The more the original sentence is reduced, the less prominent and more subsidiary does the proposition it expresses become. The following versions are on a scale of decreasing prominence:

Rocks are composed of a number of different substances which are called minerals.
Rocks are composed of a number of different substances called minerals.
Rocks are composed of a number of different substances (minerals).

When one sentence is thus incorporated into another it naturally loses its independent illocutionary force. That is to say, S2 on its own functions as an identification or a naming, and if we allow it to remain independent it is because we judge that (for the reader we are assuming) it is necessary to divide up what we want to say into two units of information: the first conveyed through the general statement of S1 and the second through the identification or naming of S2. Thus, modifying the propositional structure of the discourse has consequences for its illocutionary effect.

With this in mind, let us consider S4, S5 and S6. As was pointed out earlier, it seems natural to combine these three sentences to form one. One reason why it seems natural is that all three sentences fulfil the same illocutionary function: they are all examples of the classification according to chemical composition mentioned in S3. In other words, their significance as part of the illocutionary development of the discourse is that they take on a particular relationship with the proposition expressed in S3. Unless we can be sure that the reader recognizes this, then we run the risk of presenting him with incoherent discourse. We can mark this relationship with a coherence marker like 'for example':

For example, some are oxides, some are sulphides and some are silicates.

Alternatively, we might combine these three sentences with S3 in the following manner:

Minerals are classified according to their chemical composition: some are oxides, some are sulphides, some silicates.

If we combine the sentences like this, then again we indicate an illocutionary relationship between the propositions: those of S4, S5 and S6 appear as exemplification of the statement made in S3. To leave these sentences as they are is to represent each proposition as independent with the possibility of having its own illocutionary force. We should note also that once an illocutionary relationship is indicated, then the reader is directed to a discovery of propositional links. Even if he does not know that oxides, sulphides and silicates are terms referring to chemical composition, he will be led to infer this by the fact that the propositions of S4, S5 and S6 are represented as examples.

The re-arrangement of propositional content, then, has illocutionary implications. This is further illustrated by S7. We noted earlier that the shifting of the constituents of this sentence to make a more satisfactory given-new sequence yielded a rather suspect sentence. We can now see that this is because the rearrangement of the propositional content does not lead to an acceptable illocutionary act: what is wrong with the sentence is that it is difficult to see how it would be used meaningfully. To demonstrate this we might set it alongside another sentence of similar form:

The most important minerals in the earth are ores.
Minerals from which we extract metals are ores.

The form of the first sentence indicates that it is being used to express a general statement about ores. A reorganization of the proposition does not alter its illocutionary force:

Ores are the most important minerals in the earth.

This variant may or may not be more appropriate for propositional development in the discourse, but it remains a general statement about ores. If we consider the original version of S7, we see that the form there indicates that the sentence functions as a *definition* of ores. Now the point about a definition, of course, is that the term to be defined is given and the expression which does the defining is new. If the proposition is re-organized so that this given-new arrangement is reversed, then it can no longer function as a definition: we are no longer explaining a term already given, we are introducing a new term to identify or name something already known. In other words, the re-arrangement alters the force of the proposition from definition to identification, or naming. The reason why we feel the need to introduce the lexical item 'call' into the revised version of S7 is because we wish to mark overtly the fact that the proposition now has this illocutionary force, in just the same way as has S2. It might be noted in passing that the argument just presented also explains the oddity of:

Ores are called minerals from which we extract metals.

We come finally to S8. It has already been observed that with respect to propositional development we might expect that 'gold', not having been previously mentioned, would most naturally appear as new information at the end of the sentence. Why, then, does it seem more natural to have it appear at the beginning? The reason is that we recognize S8 as having the illocutionary function of example in this particular context. There are two ways in which we might indicate this. We could, on the one hand, alter the form of the proposition to read something like:

One of these is gold.
One of these ores is gold.
One of these minerals is gold.

Such an alteration has the effect of placing 'gold' in its appropriate position as new information. On the other hand, we can leave the propositional arrangement unchanged and insert an indicator of illocutionary function:

Gold, for example, is an ore.

The use of the indicator 'for example' makes it clear that 'gold' is not in fact altogether new since it is an example of something that has already been referred to: the indicator necessarily lends it something of the character of given information.

It seems clear, then, that the organization of propositional content so as to achieve cohesion has certain illocutionary consequences. Given our original set of sentences, there are a number of ways in which we can modify their structure so that the propositions are carried forward from one sentence to the next. Which way we choose will depend partly on how much we think the reader can infer for himself but it will also depend on what the information we are providing is meant to count as, on what function we want the propositions to have. So far we have been considering the illocutionary consequences of organizing the given set of sentences in the order in which they were presented. Other consequences arise from altering this order. We can, for example, achieve cohesion by re-ordering as follows:

Discourse B   Rocks are composed of a number of different substances. Some are oxides, some are sulphides and some are silicates. These substances are called minerals. Minerals are classified according to their chemical composition. Those from which we extract metals are called ores. Gold, for example, is an ore.

This arrangement obviously not only changes the order in which the information is presented but also alters what the sentences count as in terms of illocutionary function. With reference to the original order we can say that S1 functions as a general statement which prepares the way for the identification of the main topic to be discussed, expressed in S2. S3 then functions as another general statement, which introduces the notion of classification which is then exemplified in S4, S5 and S6. If we adopt the different order of the version given above, however, these functions change. The second sentence (previously S4, S5 and S6) functions now as an exemplification of the different substances mentioned in the first sentence. This means that the fourth sentence (previously S3) loses its value as a statement introducing the notion of classification. The classification has already been made so that S3 serves now as a clarification of the significance of what is said in the second and third sentences in this version. In other words, the fact that minerals are classified according to their chemical composition is presupposed by what has preceded here so that what S3 now does is to provide a kind of parenthetical check that the reader has indeed inferred this. We might make the function of this sentence clear by adding an indicator as follows:

That is to say, minerals are classified according to their chemical composition.

Or the discourse could develop from the third sentence in this version in the following way:

Since minerals are classified according to their chemical composition . . .

There are other re-arrangements we could make. We could, for example, have appropriate forms of S7 and S8 follow immediately on from S1 and S2:

Discourse C Rocks are composed of a number of different substances. These are called minerals. Minerals from which we extract metals are called ores. Gold, for example, is an ore. Minerals are classified according to their chemical composition. Some are oxides, some are sulphides and some are silicates.

Re-ordering in this case represents S7 as an identification of a particular class of minerals (those from which metals can be extracted) and S8 as an example of such a class, before we get a statement (expressed through S3) of how minerals are classified in general. The effect of this is to change the direction of discourse development. In the versions previously given (Discourse A and Discourse B) there is a movement towards a discussion of ores, mention of the more general classification serving as a lead-in to this topic. But in Discourse C reference to ores is made as an aside to the main theme, a kind of parenthetical comment.

2.7   Conventions of coherence

We can then arrange our original sentences in a variety of ways to yield a number of different versions. In each case we can be said to have achieved cohesion to the extent that we have arranged for propositional content to be conveyed from sentence to sentence. But the different versions function differently: to alter the arrangement is to alter the illocutionary character of the discourse. Although they can all be said to be 'saying the same thing', they are not all *doing* the same thing. Are they, then, all equally coherent? That is to say, is the illocutionary development equally acceptable in each case?

To answer this question we have to return to the point made earlier in this chapter. When using language for normal communicative purposes, the writer (or speaker) draws on what he assumes to be a common knowledge of usage to provide clues to his intended meaning. In doing this, he makes assumptions about the capacity of the reader (or hearer) for inferring propositional content that is not explicitly stated and illocutionary value which is not explicitly indicated. Part of this capacity has to do with quite general interpretative strategies which all language users bring to bear for making sense of language use.[4] Among such strategies are: assume the writer has something informative to convey, relate what he says to what you already know, if the writer does not remind you of something, assume that it is not important, assume that if one thing is said after another the two things are related in some way, assume that something expressed in a subordinate sentence is intended to be less prominent than something expressed in a main sentence, and so on. Part of the capacity for inference, however, has to do with more specific sets of conventions associated with particular kinds of discourse. We learn, for example, that business letters take a certain form, that experiments in the laboratory are written up in a certain way, and so on. A discourse is coherent to the extent that we recognize it as representative of normal language use, to the extent that we can accept the sequence of illocutionary acts as conforming to known conventions.

With regard to the three versions we have created, we can judge their relative coherence by invoking our knowledge of the conventions which inform the kind of discourse which they most closely resemble. Thus we might say that Discourse A is to be preferred to Discourse B and

C because it resembles the kind of description to be found in textbooks in which there is a progression from the general to the particular in a gradual lead-in to a specific topic. Discourses B and C are less coherent because both of them exhibit a disturbance in this progression by the insertion of a parenthetical comment: in B this comment projects the reader backwards to expand on something previously discussed and in C it leads him off on a tangent away from the main theme. To the extent that this kind of disruption does not normally occur in discourse of this kind, these versions are incoherent. Another way of putting this is to say that these versions are more difficult to process: a greater strain is put on the reader's interpretative strategies because he cannot refer to known conventions as a guide.

Coherence, then, is measured by the extent to which a particular instance of language use corresponds to a shared knowledge of conventions as to how illocutionary acts are related to form larger units of discourse of different kinds. Confronted with a piece of language we can judge how coherent it is as a description, a technical report, a legal brief, an explanation and so on. If we are not familiar with the conventions, then the language is incoherent to a degree corresponding with our unfamiliarity. It may, of course, be cohesive: we may recognize by reference to syntactic and semantic clues how the propositions relate to each other. What we do not recognize is the illocutionary significance of the relationship. This means that if we are asked to say what the piece of language is about we cannot summarize, we can only quote.

We have seen in our manipulation of the original set of sentences that the way in which they are combined has illocutionary consequences. We can arrive at a number of cohesive versions but their acceptability as instances of discourse will depend on which version is the most coherent. To organize propositions so that they link up with each other is not enough: they must link in such a way as to provide for a satisfactory illocutionary relationship. Before drawing final conclusions from the observations in this chapter it might be useful to illustrate the points I have just been making by briefly considering another set of sentences.

2.8 Deriving discourse by arrangement: another example

Instead of beginning with a set of contrived sentences we will take an actual instance of discourse and present its constituent orthographic sentences in random order. In our previous exercise we were applying our knowledge of language use to the task of creating discourse out of a set of abstract linguistic units: we were trying to simulate the encoding process. In this exercise we apply this knowledge to the interpretation of actual instances of use: we try to simulate the decoding process. Whereas before we approached discourse from the 'composition' point of view, we now approach it from the 'comprehension' point of view. These are the sentences:

1. Electro-plating is used widely in industry for a number of reasons.
2. Watch-cases and cutlery are often plated with silver or gold to give them a smart appearance so that they become attractive to intending buyers.
3. The anode had to be made of the metal which it was desired to transfer to the cathode, and the electrolyte had to be a suitable solution or salt of the metal.
4. Handlebars of bicycles and the shiny fittings of cars are also made attractive by means of nickel and chromium plating.
5. It is used for decoration.
6. Scientists found that many metals could be transferred from anode to cathode.
7. Then the cathode always became plated with metal from the anode.
8. Coatings of nickel, gold, silver or chromium give a nice shiny appearance to articles and make them look more expensive.
9. Copper, silver, gold, nickel, zinc and chromium can all be used in this process, which is called electro-plating.

We can begin by noting a number of cohesive signals. Thus, S3 contains the definite noun phrases 'The anode' and 'the cathode' which must be functioning anaphorically to relate to some previous mention. The same observation can be made of S7 which also contains the linking word 'then': this indicates that the event referred to in S7 follows on from some other event previously mentioned. The only sentence which contains a non-anaphoric reference to anode and cathode is S6, so we must assume that this sentence must precede S3 and S7 (though not necessarily in that order) so as to provide a first mention for the references in these sentences to relate to. S5 has the anaphoric pronoun 'it' so it must follow a sentence which contains a singular (non-human) noun phrase. The phrase 'this process' in S9 is also anaphoric: in this case more information is copied from a previous reference, which has to contain the semantic feature [+ process] in order to provide the required first mention. In S4 we find the linking word 'also' which is similar in some respects to 'then' in S7. The difference between them is that 'then' indicates that there is a chronological order in the propositions that are related whereas 'also' does not.

By reference to these overt signals of cohesion we can arrange these sentences in a number of ways. We can, for example, put them in the following order: 6–7–3–9–1–5–8–2–4. This yields the following version:

[6]Scientists found that many metals could be transferred from anode to cathode. [7]Then the cathode always became plated with metals from the

anode. [3]The anode had to be made of the metal which it was desired to transfer to the cathode and the electrolyte had to be a suitable solution or salt of the metal. [9]Copper, silver, gold, nickel, zinc and chromium can all be used in this process, which is called electro-plating. [1]Electro-plating is used widely in industry for a number of reasons. [5]It is used for decoration. [8]Coatings of nickel, gold, silver or chromium give a nice shiny appearance to articles and make them look more expensive. [2]Watch-cases and cutlery are often plated with silver or gold to give them a smart appearance so that they become attractive to intending buyers. [4]Handlebars of bicycles and the shiny fittings of cars are also made attractive by means of nickel and chromium plating.

Alternatively, we might adopt the order 6–9–7–3–1–5–2–4–8, and this gives us the following version:

[6]Scientists found that many metals could be transferred from anode to cathode. [9]Copper, silver, gold, nickel, zinc and chromium can all be used in this process, which is called electro-plating. [7]Then the cathode always became plated with metal from the anode. [3]The anode had to be made of the metal which it was desired to transfer to the cathode, and the electrolyte had to be a suitable solution or salt of the metal. [1]Electro-plating is used widely in industry for a number of reasons. [5]It is used for decoration. [2]Watch-cases and cutlery are often plated with silver or gold to give them a smart appearance so that they become attractive to intending buyers. [4]Handlebars of bicycles and the shiny fittings of cars are álso made attractive by means of nickel and chromium plating. [8]Coatings of nickel, gold, silver or chromium give a nice shiny appearance to articles and make them look more expensive.

Now although on the evidence of cohesive markers this ordering is possible, it somehow seems less satisfactory than the first. It seems odd, for example, to have S9 interposing between S6 and S7. Let us then investigate the source of this oddity. At first sight it would appear to lie in the fact that S9 introduces a tense form different from that of its neighbouring sentences: it is in the present tense whereas the sentences which precede and follow it are the past. In consequence a certain consistency or agreement is disturbed. And if we now look again at the set of sentences as a whole, we notice that three of them (3, 6 and 7) have verb phrases in the past whereas all the others have verb phrases in the present. It would seem reasonable to group the sentences together in accordance with the tense they exhibit; and since S6 introduced the references to which the anaphoric phrases 'the anode' and 'the cathode' relate (in S3 and S7) it would appear that the obvious order of the first three sentences is either 6–7–3 or 6–3–7.

But why should we assume that sentences naturally group together in accordance with tense agreement? It is true that the particular sequence we have here seems a little strange, but it is possible to have sequences which do not have tense agreement which are not strange at all. Consider the following, for example:

When an electric current is caused to flow through certain liquids they undergo chemical changes, their components being chemically separated. Faraday called this phenomenon of decomposition by the electric current 'electrolysis', and the liquid conductors which show it he called 'electrolytes'. The conduction of the current in an electrolytic solution is accompanied by a migratory movement of the parts of the dissolved substance. These parts are called 'ions' . . .

Here there is a shift from present to past tense between the first and second sentence and a shift back to present tense in the third. There is nothing incongruous about this because we can recognize that the tenses are functioning to appropriate illocutionary effect. We can see, for example, that the second sentence here is being used to make an historical reference to Faraday while at the same time introducing terms which are relevant to the description of the process in question. In other words, we recognize that the past tense does not prevent the second sentence here from functioning in part as a naming or identification and so equivalent in this respect to the fourth sentence. The past tense introduces an additional historical element but otherwise the expression 'Faraday called this x' has the same value in this particular discourse as 'These are called x'.

We can now return to the oddity of the 6–9–7–3 sequence in our passage on electro-plating. In the light of what has just been said, we might now suggest that the source of the oddity is not that a sentence exhibiting present tense interposes between two sentences exhibiting past tense, but that it is difficult to work out just how this interposed sentence is functioning in this context. What illocutionary value does it have? Positioned as it is, it would seem to have the value of a kind of parenthetical comment, an aside from the main development of the discourse which moves easily through the linking word 'then' from S6 to S7. But it is hard to see what the purpose of such an aside might be at this point. Furthermore, it is hard to see how the propositional content of S9 can justify considering it as an aside. We note that reference to silver and gold is taken up again in S2, that reference to nickel and chromium is taken up again in S4, and that reference to all four of these metals appears in S8. Far from being a parenthetical comment, S9 would appear to be central to the main development of the discourse. But this centrality is not realized in the 6–9–7–3 sequence. The oddity of this sequence lies in the fact that there is a discrepancy between what value

S9 takes on in this position and the value which is implied by its propositional content.

If we adopt this illocutionary perspective, noting not simply cohesive signals but how the propositions expressed function as part of a total communicative activity, then we can adduce good reasons for removing S9 from its position in the 6–9–7–3 sequence and placing it elsewhere. To do so makes better sense: that is to say, it results in more coherent discourse. Similarly, we can say that it is appropriate to have 6–7–3 grouped together not because they all manifest the past tense (since, as we have seen, tense is not of itself a crucial criterion for grouping) but because they together constitute a report of something occurring in the past. We now move from a consideration of individual sentences and their sequential function to the discovery of larger communication units in a discourse. If we look at the original set of unordered sentences, we can see that one group (6, 7 and 3) can be taken together as realizing a *report* of past events and that the others (except S9) can be seen as realizing the illocutionary act of an *account* of how the process previously reported is put to practical use. S9 can now be seen as an essential transition between these two main illocutionary elements: 'this process' refers to events reported in the past in S6, S7 and S3 but 'is called' (rather than 'was called') transposes the reference into the present and initiates the account to be given in the following part of the discourse. As with the statement about Faraday in the other example we considered, something referred to in the past is thus provided with present relevance.

So we can arrange our original set of sentences into two groups. One of these (consisting of S6, S7 and S3) represents a report of a process as discovered by scientists and the other (consisting of S1, S5, S8, S2 and S4) represents an account of how this process is put to practical use in industry. The question now arises as to which order the sentences would most appropriately occur within each group. As far as the first group is concerned the possibilities are 6–7–3 and 6–3–7. In the first version we produced we assumed that the former was the one to be preferred, basing this on our interpretation of 'then' as an indicator of sequential order of events: x happened (metals were transferred from anode to cathode) then y happened (the cathode became plated with metals from the anode). If we consider the 6–3–7 sequence, however, 'then' takes on a different value. S3 functions as a statement of the conditions necessary for the transference of metals referred to in S6 to take place. If S7 follows, we interpret it as a logical conclusion based on S3: If x (i.e. the anode was made of a suitable metal and the electrolyte was a suitable solution or salt) then y (the cathode always became plated with metals from the anode). S3, then, varies in illocutionary function depending on its position and this naturally has consequences for the way its proposition relates to those expressed through the other sentences.

If we take the 6–7–3 sequence, we can textualize the presuppositions which hold between S6 and S7 as follows:

Scientists found that many metals could be transferred from anode to cathode. (When metals were transferred in this way) then the cathode always became plated with metals from the anode. (For metals to be transferred in this way) the anode had to be made of the metal which it was desired to transfer to the cathode, and the electrolyte had to be a suitable solution or salt of the metal.

If on the other hand we take the 6–3–7 sequence, the presuppositions appear as follows:

Scientists found that many metals could be transferred from anode to cathode. (For metals to be transferred in this way) the anode had to be made of the metal which it was desired to transfer to the cathode, and the electrolyte had to be a suitable solution or salt of the metal. (If the anode was made of the metal to be transferred and the electrolyte was a suitable solution or salt of the metal) then the cathode always became plated with metals from the anode.

Both 6–7–3 and 6–3–7 are cohesive sequences. Our decision as to which is more coherent will depend on which seems to conform more closely to the conventions which regulate written discourse of this kind. The most natural order will be the one with which we are most familiar. I will return to this question presently. Meanwhile, let us briefly consider the ordering of the second group of sentences. The order proposed in the versions already given is 1–5–8–2–4 and 1–5–2–4–8. S1 introduces a change of theme: previously the process of electro-plating was described and now discussion shifts to its use and, as we have seen, we begin another large-scale illocutionary unit. In fact, a paragraph division would be appropriate here for that reason. S5 follows S1 quite naturally because having been informed that electro-plating is used for a number of reasons we anticipate that we shall be told about them. S5, then, functions as an example and we could make this explicit by inserting the appropriate marker:

For example, it is used for decoration.

To mark S5 in this way is to avoid arousing expectations in the reader that any other reasons will be given. The writer is not committed to talk about anything except decoration. If we were to mark S5 as follows, however:

First, it is used for decoration.
In the first place, it is used for decoration.

then the writer is committed to talk about other reasons and the reader's attention is projected forward in prediction. Following S5 we have S8, S2 and S4, all of which expand upon the notion of decoration and give it more precise specification. But they do so at different levels of generality. S8 mentions all four metals used for articles in general and S2 and S4 mention two of these metals in relation to particular articles. The relationship between S8 and S2/S4, therefore, is as follows:

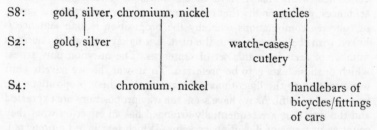

S8:   gold, silver, chromium, nickel   articles

S2:   gold, silver   watch-cases/
                                        cutlery

S4:   chromium, nickel   handlebars of
                                            bicycles/fittings
                                            of cars

S2 has to precede S4 because of the sequence marker 'also': they represent a single communicative unit which serves to give particular instances of the general statement given in S8 (as the diagram shows). But S8 does not have to precede this $2+4$ unit. If it does then $2+4$ serves as joint exemplification and the sequence as a whole is essentially deductive. But the sequence 2–4–8 is also possible. In this case, the particular instances provided in $2+4$ exemplify not S8 but S5: they illustrate the notion of decoration. S8 now takes on the value of a generalizing conclusion based on these instances: the sequence, we might say, is essentially inductive.

Given our original set of sentences, then, we can, by taking note of cohesive devices and the illocutionary functioning of the propositions expressed in the sentences, arrange them in the following ways:

$$6 - \begin{Bmatrix} 7-3 \\ 3-7 \end{Bmatrix} - 9 \ \# \ 1-5 - \begin{Bmatrix} 8-2-4 \\ 2-4-8 \end{Bmatrix}$$

report/description   account/description
of process   of use in industry

Where $\#$ indicates a possible paragraph division and the brackets indicate alternative sequences.

2.9 Summary and conclusion

I will now return to the question of relative coherence and I will do so in the context of a summary of the points that have been raised in this chapter. We began by noting that an understanding of language use requires us to recognize that in the production of a sentence we express a proposition of some sort and in the expressing of a proposition we perform an illocutionary act of some sort. Language use has to do with propositions and the acts they are used to perform. But these do not occur in isolation: they combine to form discourse. If we focus our attention on the way in which sentences are fashioned to ensure that there is a link between the propositions they express, then we are concerned with what I have called cohesion. Thus, given a set of sentences, we can modify them in a number of ways to produce a variety of cohesive combinations whereby the proposition in one sentence is linked with the proposition in the next. Let us say that we can derive a number of *texts* from this set of sentences. The question now arises: which of these texts is to be preferred. To answer this we have to shift our attention to the illocutionary functions that these propositions are being used to fulfil. As we have seen, the way propositions are expressed and the way they are sequentially arranged has an effect on what they count as in terms of illocutionary value. Which text is to be preferred, then, will depend on which one can most readily be processed by the reader as a combination of illocutionary acts which constitutes an acceptable unit of communication. That is to say, given a number of texts, all of which are cohesive, the most acceptable as a unit of discourse will be that which is most coherent.

Whereas cohesion, then, has to do with the way propositions are linked together by a variety of structural operations to form texts, coherence has to do with the illocutionary function of these propositions, with how they are used to create different kinds of discourse: reports, descriptions, explanations, and so on. The reader realizes coherence by recognizing that the propositions in the form and in the order in which they appear can be associated with illocutionary values which he accepts as appropriate. The question now arises: where does this sense of appropriacy come from?

When a child learns a language he learns at the same time how language (in general) works. He does not, quite obviously, just acquire a formal system and manifest it as usage. Inextricably bound up with his acquisition of the formal elements of his language is a development of awareness of how these elements are used in the normal business of social interaction. The child learns what it is to ask for something, to describe something, to offer excuses, to explain, and so on. He learns how interactions are managed. He learns certain basic assumptions upon which communication as a co-operative endeavour crucially depends. One of these is that the speaker (or writer) intends what he says to be informative and relevant in respect to what has been said before. Another is that meanings are not explicitly stated in sentences but have to be inferred. He learns, too, certain statistical probabilities relating to the frequency of occurrence of different linguistic elements in his language and, of particular relevance to the points made in this chapter, he learns certain common patterns of discourse development. This latter learning begins with the understanding of certain basic conversational routines, like question/answer sequences. Later the child is introduced to simple narrative sequences in the fairy stories he is told and later still, through formal education, he learns the conventions associated with factual accounts, the writing up of experiments and so on.

The sense of appropriacy which enables us to distinguish coherence in discourse derives, then, from a knowledge of communicative conventions acquired as a natural and necessary concomitant of language learning. Thus, we recognize that a particular sequence of illocutionary acts is more familiar, more normal than another and to that extent more coherent, easier to process. It would seem likely that some of the conventions which control discourse development, by reference to which coherence is recognized, are of quite general occurrence. They are, as it were, 'common sense' conventions, a basic set of ground rules. As such they serve as a frame of reference for the learning or more specific conventions associated with particular kinds of discourse.

Two further points might be made, which are, I think, of direct relevance to the teaching of foreign languages. The first is that a knowledge of these conventions derives from the learner's experience of language use. A good deal of material for the teaching of foreign languages presents the language to be learned in dissociation from a real communicative purpose in contexts devised solely as a means of teaching language. The foreign language is in this way represented as a different kind of phenomenon from the mother tongue, an artificial construct detached from the purposes for which language is normally used. It is not discourse: it is language put on display. This means that the learner is denied the opportunity of drawing on his own experience of language. If it is the case, as I have argued here, that the learning of language means acquiring the ability to handle discourse and if this crucially depends on a knowledge of conventions, then it would seem to follow that we have to link the foreign language to be learned with real contexts of use in one way or another. One such set of contexts (and here I return to points made in the previous chapter) is quite naturally provided by other subjects on the school curriculum. Part of the purpose in teaching these subjects is precisely to extend the range of the learner's knowledge of communicative conventions in his own language, to increase his capacity for recognizing coherence. An important aspect of the teaching of science, for example, is to make learners aware of what constitutes scientific explanation, or an adequate account of an experiment, and so on. Within formal education, within the reality of secondary socialization, these are real communication situations which call for genuine language use.

Teachers of physics, chemistry, biology, geography and so on may not think of themselves as language teachers, probably because they conceive of language in terms of usage, but there can be no question that they are teaching use. They are, of course, teaching it as realized through the language system of the learner's own mother tongue. And here we come to the second point I wish to make. The conventions I have been referring to are not specific to any particular language. Thus, a discourse, like, for example, a technical description, will remain the same whether it is textualized in one language or another and this accounts in large measure for the possibility of translation. Discourse differences are essentially cultural rather than linguistic. Since other subjects on the school curriculum belong to the culture of formal education which is to a large extent neutral in respect of other cultures, learners will already know some of the discourse conventions I have been referring to as a necessary consequence of knowing something of the subjects they are studying. The task of the foreign language teacher is to show how these conventions are realized through another language system. What I am suggesting is that learners already know a good deal of what we want to teach them: what we need to do is to find ways of exploiting this knowledge. By relating the teaching of another language to school subjects, the language teacher thereby extends the learners' knowledge into a different realization and so bases his teaching on the learners' own experience of language.

The suggestion is, then, that the teaching of discourse and the different conventions which determine coherence can be brought about by relating the teaching of the foreign language with the teaching of other subjects, thus bringing the teaching of another tongue into closer proximity with the teaching of the mother tongue. Our discussion of discourse in this chapter leads us to the same conclusion as was put forward in the first chapter. We can teach text recognition and production in cultural isolation without reference to any particular uses of language. But discourse can only be taught in relation to actual areas of use. Those areas of use which are immediately accessible to the language teacher and familiar to the language learner are those of other school subjects which, of their nature, must provide a systematic presentation of those conventions needed to convey the basic concepts and procedures of the subjects concerned.

These first two chapters have been concerned with what 'knowing' a language might involve. From what has been said, it clearly involves a good deal more than the ability to speak, hear, read and write correct sentences. The discussion in these chapters leads us naturally to a reconsideration of what we might mean by the 'language skills'. This is the concern of the chapter which follows.

Notes and references

1. The distinction between sentence, proposition and illocutionary act derives from:
   J. R. Searle: *Speech Acts*, Cambridge University Press, 1969. Searle himself derives the distinction from:
   J. L. Austin: *How to do things with words*, Oxford University Press, 1962.
   For a discussion of these notions with an eye to their pedagogic relevance see:
   J. P. B. Allen & H. G. Widdowson: 'Grammar and language teaching' in *ECAL Volume 2: Papers in Applied Linguistics*.
   The suggestions for further reading appended to this paper will indicate to the interested reader where he might explore these notions further.

2. The different devices available in English for achieving cohesion are exhaustively described in:
   Randolph Quirk, Sidney Greenbaum, Geoffrey Leech & Jan Svartvik: *A Grammar of Contemporary English*, Longman, 1972. Chapter 10.
   M. A. K. Halliday & Ruqaiya Hasan: *Cohesion in English*, Longman, 1976.

3. The way in which utterances which are not related formally (i.e. which are not cohesive, in my terms) are understood by recovering the communicative activity they represent (i.e. are made coherent in my terms) is discussed in:
   W. Labov: 'The study of language in its social context' in his collection of papers: *Sociolinguistic Patterns*, University of Pennsylvania Press, 1972. Section 4.
   Labov's work is discussed in:
   C. Criper & H. G. Widdowson: 'Sociolinguistics and language teaching' in *ECAL Volume 2*.

4. Recently, there has been considerable interest in interpretative strategies among philosophers of language and among sociologists adopting what is called an ethnomethodological approach to the description of language behaviour.
   The philosopher H. P. Grice discusses such strategies under the general heading of the 'co-operative principle' in his paper: 'Logic and conversation' in P. Cole & J. J. Morgan (eds): *Syntax and Semantics Volume 3: Speech Acts*, Academic Press, 1975.
   This is a collection of papers in linguistics and philosophy which represents recent thinking about how the communicative aspects of language can be formally described.

The most accessible introduction to the ideas of the ethnomethod-
ologists is:
R. Turner (ed): *Ethnomethodology*, Penguin Books, 1974.
Both the philosophical and ethnomethodological points of view are
represented in the collection of readings:
P. P. Giglioli (ed): *Language and social context*, Penguin Books, 1972.
This also contains an excerpt from the Labov paper referred to in
Note 3 and in general provides a good introduction to the issues
involved in the description of language as communication.

3 Linguistic skills and communicative abilities

3.1 The four skills

As was noted at the beginning of this book, the aims of language teaching courses are very commonly defined in terms of four skills: speaking, understanding speech (or listening), reading and writing. But what is the nature of these skills? How satisfactory is it to define the aims of language teaching by reference to them? The concern of this chapter is to consider questions of this kind and to examine how far the discussion in the previous chapters is relevant to their resolution.

Let us begin by reviewing what is usually said about these four skills. Speaking and listening are said to relate to language expressed through the aural medium and reading and writing are said to relate to language expressed through the visual medium. Another way of representing these skills is by reference not to the medium but to the activity of the language user. Thus speaking and writing are said to be active, or productive skills whereas listening and reading are said to be passive, or receptive skills. We can express these conventional notions in a simple diagram as follows:

	productive/active	receptive/passive
aural medium	speaking	listening
visual medium	writing	reading

I want to suggest that although it might be convenient to represent the language skills in this way when considering usage, it is not specially helpful, and indeed might be positively misleading, to represent them in this way when considering use. The terms aural/visual and productive/receptive refer to the way language is manifested rather than to the way it is realized in communication.

To demonstrate this, let us first note that the terms *speaking*, *reading* and *writing* are ambiguous. If, for instance, I make a remark like 'He speaks clearly' or 'She speaks slowly and distinctly' I am not using the term *speak* in the same sense as when I make remarks like 'He speaks persuasively about the need to economize' or 'She speaks frankly about her marital difficulties'. In the case of the first pair of expressions I am using the term to refer to the manner in which language is manifested and in the case of the second I am using the term to refer to the manner in which language is realized as communication. There are, in fact, two verbs *speak*: a usage verb and a use verb and they are different grammatically. Thus it would be odd to say: 'She speaks distinctly about her marital difficulties.' The same ambiguity attaches to the noun *speech*: as a mass noun it refers to usage and as a count noun it refers to use. Thus, the study of speech is the business of phoneticians whereas the study of speeches is the business of politicians. By the same token, a remark like 'His speech was clear' is ambiguous: it might mean that his delivery was distinct or it might mean that what he had to say was easy to understand. The same points can be made about the term *write* as is evident from a comparison between the expressions 'His writing is illegible' and 'His writing is logical' and from the ambiguity of the expression 'His writing is clear', which may refer either to handwriting or to style.

3.2   Activities associated with spoken language

I have said that expressions like 'He speaks clearly' and 'She writes illegibly' refer to usage. We can perhaps be a little more precise. Clarity or distinctiveness of speech refers to the manner in which the phonological system of the language is manifested, just as clarity or legibility of writing refers to the manner in which the graphological system is manifested. But now what would I be referring to if I were to say something like 'He speaks correctly'? I would probably be referring here to the grammatical system of the language and my meaning would be that what he says conforms to the accepted rules for sentence formation. So we can say that speaking in the usage sense involves the manifestation either of the phonological system or of the grammatical system of the language or both. The term used for variation in phonological manifestation is *accent* and that used for variation in grammatical manifestation is *dialect*. In both cases, speaking (with a certain accent or with a certain dialect) is simply the physical embodiment of abstract systems.

Now with reference to usage, it is perfectly true that speaking is active, or productive, and makes use of the aural medium. If we think of speaking in terms of use, however, the situation is rather different. To begin with, an act of communication through speaking is commonly performed in face to face interaction and occurs as part of a dialogue or other form of verbal exchange. What is said, therefore, is dependent on an understanding of what else has been said in the interaction. If, for example, I say something in the course of a conversation it will not be an isolated remark which has no reference to what has been said previously but will in some way derive from my understanding of what other people have already said. Speaking as an instance of use, therefore, is part of a reciprocal exchange in which both reception and production play a part. In this sense, the skill of speaking involves both receptive and productive participation.

It is conventional practice to represent speaking as the productive utilization of the aural medium. I have already suggested that speaking is only simply productive when it is conceived of in terms of usage. What I want to suggest now is that it is also only simply aural when conceived of in this way. If one thinks of speaking solely as the overt manifestation of the phonological and grammatical features of a language by means of the vocal organs, then, of course, it must be uniquely associated with the aural medium. But when we speak normally in the course of a natural communicative interaction we do not only use our vocal organs. The act of speaking involves not only the production of sounds but also the use of gesture, the movements of the muscles of the face, and indeed of the whole body.[1] All of these non-vocal accompaniments of speaking as a communicative activity are transmitted through the visual medium. When we think of speaking in this way, therefore, it is no longer true that it is associated solely with the aural medium.

If one thinks of speaking as a way in which the language system is manifested through the use of the organs of speech, then it is true that speaking is productive rather than receptive and operates through the aural rather than the visual medium. But if one thinks of speaking as exemplifying use rather than usage, as being a communicative activity, then it is both productive and receptive, both aural and visual. It will be useful at this point to mark this distinction with different terms. Let us reserve the term *speaking* for the manifestation of language as usage and refer to the realization of language as use in spoken inter-action as *talking*. We can then say that talking involves the use of both aural and visual media since it is an activity which makes use of gesture, facial expression and other paralinguistic phenomena. We can also say that it has a productive part when one participant in an interaction assumes the active role of speaker and we will refer to this productive aspect of talking as *saying*. But now what about the receptive aspect of talking? At this point we must consider the skill which is conventionally referred to as 'listening'.

When we say that we understand a piece of spoken language we can mean one of two things: either that we understand it as usage or that we understand it as use. On the one hand we recognize that the signals received by the ear relate to the phonological and grammatical system of the language concerned, that they constitute sentences, and we understand what the sentences mean as, for example, sentences of English. In one sense, then, understanding means the recognition of the signification of sentences. Let us call this kind of understanding *hearing*. To understand language as use, on the other hand, we have to recognize the communicative function of the sentences we hear, we have to recognize what acts of communication they realize. What this involves is the recognition of how the use of a particular sentence relates to what else has been said in the interaction: in other words, it is the receptive aspect of talking. We will reserve the term *listening* to refer to this activity. Hearing, then, in the sense defined here, is the activity of recognizing that signals conveyed through the aural medium constitute sentences which have a certain signification. Listening is the activity of recognizing what function sentences have in an interaction, what communicative value they take on as instances of use. Listening, therefore, in this sense, is the receptive counterpart of saying and depends on the visual as well as the aural medium.

It should be clear from this, that saying something necessarily involves speaking sentences and listening to what is said necessarily involves hearing sentences. But talking does not simply mean making use of the aural medium to speak. One can speak a sentence without saying anything and one can hear a sentence without listening to its communicative import. Speaking does not include saying and hearing does not include listening. It should be noted that from the point of view adopted here, speaking and hearing are distinct and independent activities whereas saying and listening are aspects of the one activity: talking. We might represent these different abilities in the following way:

	productive	receptive	
aural/ visual	saying	talking listening	use
aural	speaking	hearing	usage

With reference to language teaching, it will be readily agreed that, where the aim of the language course is to develop an ability to handle spoken language, what learners need ultimately to acquire is an awareness of how the language being learned is used for talking. It may be, of course, that in certain circumstances it is expedient to spend time on the teaching of speaking and hearing first before moving on to the higher level communicative ability of talking. The important thing is that teachers should accept that such a move must be made some time if their learners are really to be able to use the language in its spoken mode. In the past there has been the tendency either to ignore the kind of differences I have been discussing here, or to leave them inexplicit. The point that I would wish to make is that in making them explicit we can get a clearer idea of what is involved in learning spoken language and can begin to set up principles for teaching procedures accordingly. I do not wish to deny that there may be a place for the teaching of speaking and hearing in a language course. But it is important that we should recognize just what this teaching achieves and be careful not to confuse it with the teaching of talking.

3.3   Activities associated with written language

Let us now turn our attention to reading and writing. The first observation we might make is that whereas it is reasonable to think of saying and listening as reciprocal aspects of the one basic activity of talking, reading and writing cannot so readily be considered as reciprocal activities in quite the same sense. Most spoken discourse takes the form of an exchange whereby participants in an interaction alternately say something and listen: hence there is generally a close inter-relationship between the productive and receptive activities. In most written discourse, however, this inter-relationship does not exist: reading and writing are not typically reciprocal activities in the same way as are saying and listening. It is true that we do have written as well as spoken interactions, as in the case of an exchange of correspondence, and indeed correspondence might be considered as the larger-scale version of talking in the written mode. But there is a vast amount of written discourse that does not take the form of an exchange. Usually, what is written does not directly depend on a previous reading activity and a particular act of writing is not necessarily prompted by a particular act of reading.

Later in this chapter I shall return to the question of reciprocity and I shall suggest that another way of considering language abilities is to think of them in terms of reciprocal and non-reciprocal communication. For the present, let us agree that, in general, writing and reading are typically distinct activities in a way that saying and listening are not. The question now arises as to whether we can conclude from this that writing can be accurately described as a productive ability and reading a receptive one.

Let us approach this question by noticing that writing as a physical activity is productive in the same way as speaking is (using the term speaking in the sense previously defined). That is to say, the movement of certain bodily organs produces something perceptible to the senses.

In the case of speaking, the movements of the speech organs produce sounds which are perceived by the ear and in the case of writing, the movements of the arm and fingers (mechanically aided for me at the moment as I write this by the keys of my typewriter) produce marks which are perceived by the eye. These marks are letters which are arranged into groups to form words in accordance with the graphological system of English. I do not simply tap out letters at random. Nor do the groups of letters constituting words occur randomly: they combine to make well-formed sentences of English. So one way of describing writing is to say that it is the use of the visual medium to manifest the graphological and grammatical system of the language. That is to say, writing in one sense is the production of sentences as instances of usage. But of course I am not just producing sentences at the moment as I sit here in front of my typewriter. I could, for example, write:

The policeman caught the thief.
Where have all the flowers gone?
I am puzzled by Einstein's theory of relativity.

Here I have written three sentences and each one of them makes perfect sense in itself, each one of them has its own signification as a sentence. But if I had simply incorporated them into the paragraph without comment I am puzzled by Einstein's theory of relativity they would have made no sense at all where have all the flowers gone? It would have been assumed that they had appeared by mistake as the result of a printing error.

What I am doing as I write, then, is not just producing a sequence of English sentences. I am using sentences to create a discourse and each sentence takes on a particular value as a part of this discourse. In one sense, then, we may say that writing is the act of making up correct sentences and transmitting them through the visual medium as marks on paper. Let us call this simply *composing* and say that it corresponds with speaking in the aural medium. At the same time, writing as an activity that I am indulging in at the moment is not simply composing. What I am doing (successfully or not) is developing a discussion and arranging different points in such a way as to persuade you, the reader, that I have something worthwhile to say. What is involved in this activity? There is certainly more to it than simply putting sentences together in a sequence like wagons in a train. A good deal of time is spent going over what has previously been written and pondering on how the discourse might most effectively develop from it. Thus, what I am writing now is dependent on my recollection of what has gone before. It is also dependent on how I think what I have written so far will be understood and on what I assume to be common ground between myself, the writer, and you, the reader. In writing I also assume the reader's role. In other words, writing as use, as distinct from composing (writing as usage), can be said to be receptive in the sense that it proceeds by reference to the writer's own interpretation of what has preceded and to his assessment as to how what has been written and is being written will be received by the reader. If we regard reading as being receptive, therefore, then writing as use must be partially receptive too.

But is reading simply receptive? We can make the same point about reading as was made earlier about listening. The understanding can refer to the signification of sentences or to the value they assume in communicative use. That is to say, reading can refer to the ability to recognize sentences and their meaning as linguistic elements or it can refer to the ability to recognize how they function as parts of a discourse. The former ability is clearly the receptive analogue of composing and the visual analogue of hearing. Let us use the term *comprehending* to refer to this ability. Comprehending in this sense is the ability to recognize sentences manifested through the visual medium and to associate them with their correct signification. It corresponds with hearing in the aural medium. The question now arises as to what corresponds with listening in the aural medium.

Reading as the understanding of discourse does not simply involve the recognition of what words and sentences mean but also the recognition of the value they take on in association with each other as elements in a discourse. What happens when we read with understanding is that we actively work out what the discourse means as we go along, predicting what is to come by reference to what has preceded. Reading in this sense is a kind of accomplishment whereby a discourse is created in the mind by means of a process of reasoning. In this respect, the ability to read and the ability to write are the same and it is neutral with regard to production or reception. Essentially this ability enables us to create or re-create discourse from the resources available in the language system and, on occasions, from other conventional symbols (which I shall be discussing later on). We will call this ability, common to both writing and reading as communicative activities, *interpreting*. Interpreting, then, is the ability in the visual medium which corresponds to talking in the aural/visual medium, with the difference that in talking the productive/receptive aspects are made overt in saying and listening.

Perhaps I should make it clear at this point that I hold no particular brief for the terms I have used here to distinguish the different abilities I have been discussing. Clearly, the processing of spoken discourse also has to do with interpreting in a more general sense and one composes sentences in speaking and comprehends them in hearing. It happens that English has several terms which can be used to refer to how language is manifested and realized in speech but 'reading' and 'writing' are the only ones readily available for referring to language in its written form. For our purposes, we will restrict these latter terms to refer to the reception and production of language use respectively, thus making them correspond with saying and listening.[2]

We can now summarize the relationship between the different activities associated with the written language in the form of a diagram corresponding to the one given earlier for the activities associated with the spoken language.

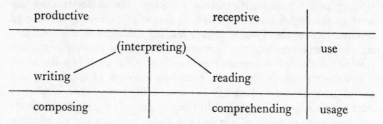

The term *interpreting* appears in parenthesis because it is a psychological process which, unlike talking, is not realized as actual social activity. Talking is overt behaviour which is open to direct observation whereas interpreting is a covert activity in the mind. At this point we return to a remark made earlier in this chapter that saying and listening are essentially reciprocal activities whereas writing and reading are not. Let us explore the implications of this.

3.4 Reciprocal and non-reciprocal activities

We say that talking is reciprocal because it takes the form of an exchange between two or more participants with each participant taking turns to say something. Any misunderstandings which arise can be cleared up in the process of the interaction and the participants rely on the 'feedback' provided by the reactions of the other interlocutors. This means that they can afford to be imprecise and inexplicit and they can clarify and modify their meanings as they go along according to how what they say is received. Talking is a kind of tactical manoeuvring. It is to be characterized as an overtly interactive manner of communicating. But of course not all spoken discourse is interactive in this way. When we listen to a speech, or a lecture, for example, we do not say anything: the communication is non-reciprocal. But this does not mean that we are being purely receptive. We actively participate in the understanding of what is said in much the same way as we actively participate in the understanding of what is written when we read. Sometimes, indeed, we do actually say things, either under our breath or out loud, thus making our activity overt. And when we listen, as when we read, we sometimes take notes. Remarks like 'Rubbish' muttered under our breath or scribbled in a margin bear witness to our participation. We may say, then, that in the non-reciprocal but interactive participation in spoken discourse there is a process analogous to interpreting in written discourse. Simply the interpretative process is not made overt as talking.

Turning now to written discourse, it is evident that although a good deal of it is non-reciprocal, writing and reading being as has been noted in large measure independent activities, some forms of written discourse are reciprocal. Consider, for example, an exchange of correspondence. This can be reasonably regarded as a written analogue of talking (although there are, of course, considerable and important differences between these two modes of exchange). Let us call the reciprocal manner of communicating in written discourse *corresponding*. Thus corresponding is the overt expression of the interpretative process in relation to written discourse just as talking is the overt expression of this process in relation to spoken discourse.

If we think of the language skills in terms of reciprocity, then, we arrive at a rather different representation of their relationship. This can be shown as follows:

	reciprocal (social activity)	non-reciprocal (psychological activity)
written mode	corresponding	interpreting
spoken mode	talking	

We have now established three ways in which the language skills might be classified. With reference to *medium*, the actual physical means whereby the language system is manifested as usage, we can specify speaking and composing as the productive skills using the aural and visual media respectively and, of course, we can also specify hearing and comprehending as their receptive counterparts. With reference to *mode*, the way in which the language system is realized as use in acts of communication, we can distinguish a written mode in which interpretation is expressed productively as writing or conducted receptively in reading and a spoken mode which is realized productively as saying and receptively as listening. Finally, with reference to *manner*, the kind of social activity involved in communication, we can distinguish the reciprocal skills of corresponding in the written mode and talking in the spoken mode and contrast these with the non-reciprocal skill of interpreting, which is the psychological process of understanding which is not made overt through physical or social activity. In the following diagram we can give a general idea of these different language skills. Those which are defined with reference to manner are in capital letters and those which are defined with reference to mode are in italics. The skills which relate simply to medium appear in ordinary print.

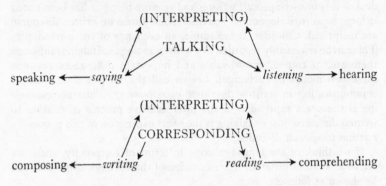

In this diagram, the sameness of typeface is meant to indicate the sameness of type of the different skills. Thus, interpreting, talking and corresponding are skills defined with reference to manner; saying, listening, writing and reading are skills defined with reference to mode; and speaking, hearing, composing and comprehending are skills which are defined with reference to medium. Medium skills have to do with how the language system is manifested as usage and manner and mode skills have to do with how the system is realized as use. The arrows on the diagram are intended to show dependency. Thus, you can speak a sentence without saying anything and you can compose a sentence without writing anything. Similarly, you can hear what a sentence means in terms of its signification without listening to what value it has as an act of communication and you can comprehend the signification of a written sentence without recognizing what it counts as in the context of a particular piece of written discourse. Saying something, however, necessarily involves speaking a sentence, and writing something necessarily involves composing a sentence. Similarly, you can say something without talking, as when you deliver a speech or a sermon, but you cannot talk without saying and listening. And you can write something without corresponding, as when you write a report (or as I am now writing this book) but you cannot correspond without writing and reading. Interpreting is represented here as the highest level skill: it is the ability to process language as communication and it underlies all language use. You cannot talk or correspond without interpreting but you can interpret without talking or corresponding, as when you attend a lecture (where interpreting underlies listening) or read a newspaper (where interpreting underlies reading) or produce an essay (where interpreting underlies writing) or deliver an after-dinner address (where interpreting underlies saying).

3.5 Linguistic skills and communicative abilities

So far in this chapter I have used the terms *skill* and *ability* interchangeably. It will be useful at this point to make a distinction. Let us say that those skills which are defined with reference to medium (speaking, hearing, composing and comprehending) are *linguistic skills*. They refer to the way in which the language system is manifested, or recognized to be manifested, as usage. And we will refer to those skills which are defined with reference to the manner and mode in which the system is realized as use as *communicative abilities*. Communicative abilities embrace linguistic skills but not the reverse.[3]

The rather elaborate representation of these skills and abilities that has been developed in this chapter is in sharp contrast to the simple scheme which served as the starting point of our discussion. The question now is: how relevant is such an elaboration? There is little point in complicating matters in this way unless it can be shown that this complication has some bearing on the learning and teaching of languages. I think that it has, and it is to the pedagogic implications of this discussion that we now turn our attention.

To begin with, it will be generally acknowledged that the ultimate aim in language learning is to acquire communicative competence, to interpret, whether this is made overt in talking or corresponding or whether it remains covert as a psychological activity underlying the ability to say, listen, write and read. I assume that the issue is not whether this is the aim of language learning but how this aim is to be achieved. It will also be generally agreed, perhaps, that traditionally the focus of attention has been on the linguistic skills and that it has commonly been supposed that once these are acquired in reasonable measure the communicative abilities will follow as a more or less automatic consequence. What evidence we have, however, suggests that this is not the case: the acquisition of linguistic skills does not seem to guarantee the consequent acquisition of communicative abilities in a language. On the contrary, it would seem to be the case that an overemphasis on drills and exercises for the production and reception of sentences tends to inhibit the development of communicative abilities. This is not meant to imply that such drills and exercises are not necessary. As was pointed out earlier, the abilities include the skills: one cannot acquire the former without acquiring the latter. The question is: how can the skills be taught, not as a self-sufficient achievement but as an aspect of communicative competence? How can skills be related to abilities, usage to use?

These are questions we shall be considering in the second part of the book. For the present, let us try to establish as clearly as possible, with reference to the discussion in the preceding chapter, just what is the nature of these communicative abilities. Essentially they are ways of creating or re-creating discourse in different modes. As was suggested in the last chapter this activity involves inferring what propositions sentences are being used to express and how they inter-relate. It involves also the ability to infer what illocutionary acts these propositions are being used to perform and how these combine in a coherent way. In brief, it involves an understanding of the communicative value of linguistic elements in context and this is based on a knowledge of how these elements may serve as clues which can be interpreted by reference to shared conventions of communication. To illustrate this, let us consider the following short passage:

[1]Merchants in the Middle Ages who traded in spices, silk and carpets had no knowledge of the lands from which they came. [2]For them, the East remained a mystery. [3]The region was a remote place, ruled over by the fabulous Prester John. [4]This ruler was said to be immensely wealthy, far wealthier than any Western monarch, and the commodities that found their way into European market places were an indication of his riches.

To make sense of this we have to infer the appropriate value for certain linguistic elements. In S(entence)1, for example, 'they' could refer to either of the two noun phrases 'merchants in the Middle Ages' and 'spices, silk and carpets'. The signification of the word specifies only that it copies plurality from a preceding reference but here there are two or more possibilities and we have to infer which one is being referred to by this pronoun. Again, consider the noun phrase 'the East' in S2. Its signification as recorded in a dictionary might be 'lands in the eastern hemisphere' or 'Asian countries' or something of that kind. But in this context we recognize that the phrase carries with it a reference from the preceding sentence and we infer a value for it which is an extension of its dictionary meaning: something like 'lands in the eastern hemisphere where spices, silk and carpets came from'. This extended reference is again taken up by the expression 'the region' in S3. In these examples, interpreting involves inferring meaning by reference across adjacent sentences but relationships may have to be established between propositions which are not so juxtaposed. In S4, for example, the noun phrase 'the commodities that found their way into (European) market places' has to be interpreted as relating back to the expression in S1. 'Merchants (in the Middle Ages) who traded in spices, silk and carpets'.

Establishing this link has the further consequence of confirming that the merchants referred to are European merchants. All of this is, of course, self-evident enough to an efficient reader and I do not mean to suggest that we are conscious of our inferences when we make sense of a passage like this. Nor do I wish to imply that the information in a passage is only accessible by the kind of inference I have been illustrating: we may relate a reference directly to our knowledge of the world and the passage may simply serve to call to mind something we already know. But the taking of a short cut presupposes a knowledge of the longer route: the practised reader has the interpreting ability I am trying to investigate here even though he may not be conscious of its operation and may not need to exercise it fully on all occasions. And the language learner has somehow to acquire it.

Discussion of this passage so far has concentrated on the cohesive links which are clues to propositional development. Interpretation also involves a recognition of illocutionary value. Consider, for example, S3. In a different context the proposition it is used to express would take on the value of a statement of fact, as in the following:

China in the Middle Ages had very little contact with Europe. The region was a remote place, ruled over by the fabulous Prester John.

But in the passage we are considering it has a different value. S1 and S2 count as statements of fact about the merchants in the Middle Ages and their knowledge (or lack of it), but S2 shifts the perspective from the historian's point of view to the merchants'. In consequence we recognize that S3 functions not as a statement of fact but as a statement of belief. Thus the expression 'for them', which indicates the condition under which the proposition expressed is true, is also a signal that the perspective changes and we infer the appropriate illocutionary value for S3 accordingly. If we take the propositional content of S1 and S3, we can derive from them the following statements:

Merchants in the Middle Ages traded in spices, silk and carpets.
The lands in the East were ruled over by Prester John.

The first of these is true as a historical statement. The second, however, is not.

3.6 Retrospective and prospective interpretation

I have suggested that the illocutionary value of S3 is derived retrospectively by association with S2. Earlier I tried to show how propositional value is also retrospectively derived by the reader relating anaphoric expressions to the relevant previous mention. But interpretation works prospectively as well. Consider S2 again. The anaphoric pronoun 'them' directs the reader to what has gone before and his retrospection enables him to realize its value. But the proposition which is expressed also stimulates expectation of what is to follow. The reader is equipped with a knowledge of certain conventions (already discussed in Chapter 2) which he assumes the writer shares. Thus, among other things he expects that the writer will be informative and relevant. So when the writer uses a separate sentence to say that the East was a mystery the reader is inclined to predict that he will be told why it was a mystery or in what the mystery consists: his attention is projected forward. The proposition expressed in S2, then, not only has a retrospective value in that it relates to what has preceded, but it also has a prospective value in that it sets up predictions as to what proposition is to follow. Let us consider another example. Suppose that the following is the beginning of a passage:

The early peoples of the eastern Mediterranean believed that, situated somewhere far south of the Mediterranean Sea, there was an Earthly Paradise from which there flowed four mighty rivers.

What do we expect might come next? Knowing the common conventions of communication, we assume that the writer is not just throwing off a mention of the four mighty rivers as a random bit of information: we predict, therefore, that having introduced this topic, and in particular having used the evaluative term 'mighty', the writer will tell us more in what follows. The expression 'four mighty rivers', then, has prospective value in that it leads the reader to predict a development from it. So we expect that the writer will tell us more about these rivers, and why they are mighty. Sure enough, the passage continues as follows:

These watered the whole Earth and were, accordingly, the source of all fruitfulness. To them the most important of these rivers was the Nile, for on its flood-waters depended the prosperity of Egypt. The Nile remained a river of mystery until the 19th century.

We might pause here and again ask what we imagine is likely to follow next. The term 'mystery', here, as in the previous passage, and like the term 'mighty' earlier on in this passage, provokes the curiosity and we predict that our curiosity will be satisfied in what is to follow, assuming again that the writer shares with us the conventions which ensure co-operation in language use. So we expect to be told why the Nile was such a mystery, we predict that what comes next will count as an explanation. Sure enough, the passage continues as follows:

In the 1,700 miles of its course upstream from the sea it received no tributary, it crossed a desert region of practically no rainfall—and yet it carried volumes of water in regular and heavy floods. Its upper course was unexplored and its source unknown. Little wonder that to the people of Egypt it was sacred.

3.7 Assimilation and discrimination

The interpreting ability which underlies effective reading, then, involves the realization of propositional and illocutionary value by reference to what has preceded and the prediction of the propositional and rhetorical value of what is to follow. But that is not the whole story. What we have been discussing is the immediate process of interpretation whereby we assimilate meaning. But reading is a matter of discrimination as well as assimilation. When we read we evaluate the relative significance of the information we take in, we recognize that some of it, for example, has only a supporting role to play: it is there to facilitate the conveying of the main message, so that once it has fulfilled that function it can be set aside. It is this ability to discriminate relative significance which enables us to take notes and write summaries. To illustrate how this discriminating ability works we might consider the following passage:[4]

[1]Pliny the Elder in his highly unreliable Natural History gives directions for distinguishing a genuine diamond. [2]It should be put, he says, on a blacksmith's anvil and smitten with a heavy hammer as hard as possible: if it breaks it is not a true diamond. [3]It is likely that a good many valuable stones were destroyed in this way because Pliny was muddling up hardness and toughness. [4]Diamond is the hardest of all substances, but it is quite brittle, so that, even if one could get it cheaply in large pieces it would not be a very useful structural substance.

Two questions arise: what is this passage about (that is to say, what proposition is expressed) and what is the writer doing (that is to say, what illocutionary act is being performed). Now we might suggest that the passage is about Pliny the Elder and his test for discovering whether a stone is a diamond or not and if the passage had ended with S2 one would not wish to quarrel with this suggestion. But S3 marks the transition to another topic, which is developed in S4, and which has to do with the properties of diamonds. As we read, we recognize that what is said about Pliny in S1 and S2 serves as an introductory setting to prepare the reader for the main point of information: it serves a facilitating function. Discriminating in this way, we can see that the passage is about the hardness and toughness of diamonds and about their structural usefulness.

In similar fashion (turning now to illocutionary function) we might note that S1 and S2 count as reports of what Pliny said and S3 is a comment on it. In answer to a question about what the writer is doing we might in consequence hazard the suggestion that he is reporting and commenting on certain pronouncements of Pliny the Elder. But as I have already pointed out, in the context of the passage as a whole the report in S1 and S2 serves an introductory purpose and S3 marks the transition to the main theme. It now becomes plain that what the writer is doing in the passage is making a distinction between the properties of hardness and toughness in diamonds and explaining what is meant by a useful structural substance. The report and the comment in the early part of the passage are only there in support of these basic communicative purposes.

If we were asked to provide a summary of this passage, then, it would not be very satisfactory to do so as follows:

The author tells of Pliny the Elder's advice for testing whether stones are diamonds or not and explains why it is mistaken.

What we need is something like the following:

The author explains why diamonds are not useful structural material by pointing out that although they are hard they are not tough.

The recognition that interpreting is both an assimilating and a discriminating process, that propositions vary in prominence and function as the reader proceeds, is of direct relevance to the pedagogic practice of asking so called 'comprehension questions'. These have a tendency to concentrate on the immediate assimilating aspect of reading and one proposition is represented as being as significant as another without regard to how it functions. Thus a likely set of comprehension questions for the passage we have been considering might be something like:

1. Where are Pliny's directions for distinguishing a genuine diamond to be found?
2. What did he suggest one should do to test whether a stone was a diamond or not?
3. What did he say would happen if a stone which was not a real diamond was hit with a hammer?
4. Was Pliny wrong? Why?

Not only do questions of this sort fail to direct the learner towards a discovery of the main point of the passage but they may actually discourage him from acquiring the ability to do so. They can be quite legitimately used to develop the assimilating process but they need to be supplemented by questions, or other forms of exercise, which will develop the discriminating process.

3.8 Non-verbal communication

I shall be dealing with so called 'comprehension questions' in the following chapter. Meanwhile, another point should be made about interpreting. It is that interpreting does not just operate on the verbal text but on discourse as a whole, which is not purely verbal. Most discourse includes a verbal component, but the verbal component, which can be isolated and treated as usage, is only a part, and a dependent part, of the communicative event. Spoken discourse illustrates this quite clearly. As has already been indicated, communication through the spoken mode is not realized by speaking, which is by definition only verbal, but by saying, which employs such paralinguistic devices as gesture, facial expression and so on, which are conveyed through the visual medium. It was for this reason that talking, the overtly realized activity of interpreting spoken communication, was related to saying and listening rather than to speaking and hearing. Speaking and hearing relate only to the verbal elements of language manifested by means of the aural medium. The communicative abilities of saying and listening, on the other hand, operate on both the verbal and the non-verbal features of discourse.

Consider now written discourse. Although a good deal of it is purely verbal and although the paralinguistic features of spoken discourse are not directly recorded in the written mode, it is quite common to find non-verbal elements in written discourse. If one opens a book on geography, for example, one finds maps and diagrams embedded in the verbal text. A pamphlet of instructions will commonly contain drawings with arrows to indicate pictorially how the instructions are to be carried out. Scientific papers will express information through diagrams and algebraic formulae. In a very wide range of written discourse we will find such non-verbal devices as drawings, flow-charts, tables, graphs, charts and so on which are incorporated into the discourse and relate to the actual verbal text to form a cohesive and coherent unit of communication. The interpreting of written discourse involves the processing of these non-verbal elements and a recognition of their relationship to the verbal text. We cannot say that we have understood a piece of spoken discourse by listening if we have only paid attention to what is spoken and we cannot say that we have understood a piece of written discourse by reading if we have only paid attention to what is verbally composed when the discourse contains non-verbal elements as well.

The point that I am making is that the communicative abilities operate on everything that is communicative in the discourse as a whole. The linguistic skills, on the other hand, can by definition only operate on what is verbally manifested. As has already been observed, language teaching has traditionally concentrated on the linguistic skills and the non-verbal aspects of discourse have tended to be neglected.

3.9   Summary and conclusion

Let us now once again relate these observations about the non-verbal aspects of communication to the suggestion that was made in the preceding chapters that language as use might most effectively be taught by associating the teaching of language with other subjects in the school curriculum. The first point to be made is that the content of these subjects is represented by written discourse which abounds in the kind of non-verbal devices which we have been discussing. Indeed, part of the learning of these subjects is in the understanding of how such non-verbal devices work, and they might be said to constitute essential features of their basic rhetoric. In a science textbook, for example, we find formulae and conventional diagrams which pupils have to interpret in their reading and writing as a part of their learning of science. To this extent, pupils have acquired or are acquiring communicative abilities already. What has still to be done is to associate these communicative abilities, previously related to linguistic skills operating on their own language, to the linguistic skills related to the foreign language. I do not wish to suggest that this is an easy task. But it is certainly easier than attempting to teach communicative abilities in a foreign language in isolation from the pupils' already acquired experience of language use. It is easier and more relevant to the learner's purposes. I believe that many of the difficulties that learners have had in the past derive directly from the teaching that has been imposed upon them. This has tended to represent language, to misrepresent language, as a set of formal elements to be manifested and apprehended by means of linguistic skills outside a real communicative context and without a real communicative purpose. Such a model of language is remote from the learner's own experience and it is no wonder that he has difficulties in acquiring it.

The suggestion is, then, that we can make use of the learners' knowledge of non-verbal aspects of discourse, and of their ability to interpret them, as a means of linking their communicative abilities in their own language to a realization of these abilities in the language they are learning. To put it another way, we need to remove these abilities from a dependence on linguistic skills in the mother tongue and associate them with linguistic skills in the foreign language. We thereby represent (without misrepresenting) foreign language learning not as the acquisition of abilities which are new but as the transference of the abilities that have already been acquired into a different means of expression. If this is done successfully, of course, the learner can go on to extend the range of his communicative abilities through the foreign language without reference to his mother tongue.

This concludes the first part of this book. In it I have tried to investigate as carefully as I can certain issues relating to the nature of language and the language user's competence which (it seems to me) must be considered when one seriously undertakes the teaching of language as communication. I would not wish to claim that I have resolved these issues but only that I have (to some extent at least) brought them out into the open where they can be debated. The teaching of language is a very complex affair and language teachers in the past have not always been encouraged to inquire into the nature of its complexity. In consequence they have frequently fallen prey to fashionable orthodoxies. I think it is important to recognize that language teaching is a theoretical as well as a practical activity, that effective teaching materials and classroom procedures depend on principles deriving from an understanding of what language is and how it is used. In this first part of the book my concern has been with theory. In the second part I turn my attention to some of the practical implications that would appear to arise from it.

Notes and references

1. As Abercrombie puts it: 'We speak with our vocal organs, but we converse with our entire bodies.' See:

   David Abercrombie: 'Paralinguistic communication' in *ECAL Volume 1*, Chapter 6.

   A number of papers dealing with the non-vocal aspects of spoken interaction appear in:

   John Laver & Sandy Hutcheson (eds), *Communication in Face to Face Interaction*, Penguin Books, 1972, Part 4.

2. This proliferation of terms is unfortunate but I do not see how it can be avoided since we need terms to mark the distinctions I am trying to make. The distinctions themselves may be open to dispute, but that is another matter. Another difficulty about the particular terms I am using is that I am requiring the reader to disregard their signification in favour of the value I attribute to them by definition in this discussion. This might be especially difficult with a term like 'interpreting' which is normally understood as having to do with reception rather than production. The reader might find it easier to adjust to my sense of the term by thinking of the activity of the professional interpreter which is both receptive and productive and can be regarded as an overt expression of the underlying ability which I am using the term 'interpreting' to refer to.

3. Notice that if one defines skills in this way as distinct from (though

related to) abilities, then there is a case for adopting the conventional 'behaviourist' view that they can be acquired by mechanical repetition as a set of habits. The danger is that if skills are not clearly defined in this way, it might be assumed that abilities can also be acquired like this. Consider, for example, the following comment: 'The single paramount fact about language learning is that it concerns, not problem solving, but the formation and performance of habits.' N. Brooks: *Language and Language Learning*, Harcourt, Brace & World, 1960, p. 46.

'Behaviourist' attitudes like this to the learning of language are passed under critical review in Wilga Rivers: *The Psychologist and the Foreign Language Teacher*, Chicago University Press, 1964.

A thorough discussion, from a psychological point of view, of the kind of issues I raise in this chapter with regard to skills and abilities, is to be found in a later book by Rivers:

Wilga Rivers: *Teaching Foreign Language Skills*, University of Chicago Press, 1968.

In general one might say that a behaviourist orientation to psychology will tend to describe language learning activity in terms of skills and a cognitive orientation will tend to describe it in terms of abilities.

4. This passage was drawn to my attention by H. K. Nyyssonen and my comments on it are based on his observations.

4 Comprehending and reading

4.1 Preview

In the first part of this book I have tried to clarify what in general is involved in using language as an instrument of communication, and to establish certain theoretical terms of reference. What I want to do in this second part of the book is to bring this discussion to bear on the practical concerns of language teaching. I shall do this by examining a number of procedures commonly employed by teachers and textbook writers and suggesting some ways in which these might be modified or extended to develop the communicative abilities discussed in the preceding chapter.

In what follows I shall restrict my attention to written discourse, to the development of the communicative abilities of reading (in this chapter) and writing (in the one that follows) and the associated skills of comprehending and composing. But although these activities will occupy the centre of the stage, much of what I say will, I hope, have relevance by implication to the skills and abilities relating to language in its spoken form. It was argued in the preceding chapter that the ability to interpret underlies all language use: it is consistent with this argument to claim that what I shall have to say about reading and writing will have some bearing on the other communicative abilities. The relationships between skills and abilities and between manner, mode and medium constitute common problems in the teaching of both written and spoken language.

In this present chapter I intend to concentrate on the relationship between reading and comprehending and I shall be looking at ways in which reading passages are generally treated and at possible alternative treatments. The chapter that follows will then focus on the relationship between writing and composing and in the last chapter I shall try to show how the mutual dependency of both reading and writing on the underlying interpreting ability might be given pedagogic recognition by the design of an integrated methodological scheme.

4.2 The reading passage as dependent exemplification

The presentation of language through reading passages (with appended comprehension questions) is a well-established and very familiar pedagogic practice. But what is the purpose of such passages? When they appear in structurally graded courses they seem primarily to be used as a vehicle for usage, to consolidate a knowledge of structure and vocabulary that has already been introduced and to extend this knowledge by incorporating into the passages examples of whatever elements of usage come next in the course. In this case, the passage is intended as a manifestation of selected parts of the language system and in consequence they frequently exhibit an abnormally high occurrence of particular structures. It has something of the character of a display case and its value as discourse is decreased accordingly. The effectiveness of passages of this kind as a means of manifesting a restricted set of elements from the language system is achieved at the expense of a normal realization of the system as use. Even when there is an attempt to introduce features to lend a verisimilitude of normality these features do not merge into the passage in a natural way but only serve to accentuate its abnormality. Sometimes, for example, reading passages are cast in the form of dialogue but the dialogue is so obviously a device for displaying usage that they bear little resemblance to actual talking.

It should be noted, however, that although passages of this kind function essentially as exemplification of linguistic elements, these elements occur in sentences which are combined to form larger units. That is to say, these passages necessarily exhibit that aspect of use that was referred to previously as cohesion. Interestingly, however, this only seems to make their abnormality as discourse more apparent. The reason for this is that, as was demonstrated in Chapter 2, cohesion is a device for signalling propositional development and this is inextricably bound up with illocutionary development; one does not employ cohesive markers just to idle away the time, one does so to ensure that propositions relate to each other in a meaningful way, and one does not just ensure this for its own sake but as part of the business of achieving coherent discourse. In other words, cohesion just does not occur in normal circumstances unless it serves as a contributing factor to coherence. What is odd about the kind of reading passage we are considering now is that it exhibits cohesion in isolation from a communicative purpose, detached from its normal function as a means of creating discourse. If the language to be taught were presented as a set of sentences there would be no difficulty of this kind since we would not be tempted to interpret them as use, but once sentences are combined to form passages, then they take on the appearance of use and masquerade, as it were, as discourse. But in most cases the passages produced in structurally graded syllabuses correspond to no normal conventions of language use and are not representative of any kind of discourse. To the extent that they exhibit cohesion we might say that they are *texts*, but they are deficient as discourses to the extent that they lack the implication of actual use.

I do not wish to imply by this that passages of this sort are to be con-
demned out of hand: they can, no doubt, be made to serve a useful
purpose. But it is important (or so it seems to me) to understand as
clearly as we can what kind of language data they represent and so to
appreciate the limitations of their usefulness. The presentation of
language for language learning purposes is bound, I think, to be a misrepresentation in some degree. The language learner can scarcely be
unaware that this is so: we count on his willing suspension of disbelief.
The question is what kind of misrepresentation leads the learner most
readily towards an ability to cope with real language: what kind exerts
least strain on the learner's tolerance. How can we contrive to make the
language we present less of a contrivance? This seems to me to be a
central issue in language teaching pedagogy and I shall return to it
again later on.

4.3 The reading passage as independent 'comprehension piece'

So far I have been referring to reading passages which appear as parts of
a structurally graded course. They also appear, of course, independently
presented in practice books of reading comprehension exercises. Here
the structural constraints are less severe in that the passages do not have
to be fitted into slots within a graded syllabus. The possibility of approxi-
mating to actual discourse is accordingly increased. It is true that many
such books work within a restricted set of structures and vocabulary
items, but they are free of the necessity of manifesting new language
items, so the distortion due to excessive exemplification can be avoided.
Whereas passages incorporated within a graded course are used principally to display language as usage, those which appear in collections of
'comprehension pieces' are intended as demonstrations of language as
use. The learner is invited to read them as discourse and not simply as
exemplificatory texts. Two questions arise: How far do they actually
approximate to discourse? How far do they need to do so to be effective?

It is convenient to approach an answer to these questions by first
distinguishing three kinds of passage which commonly occur in the kind
of collections we have been discussing. I will call them *extracts*,
simplified versions, and *simple accounts* and we will consider each of
them in turn.

4.3.1 *Extracts: the problem of authenticity*

The extract is quite simply a piece of genuine discourse, an actual
instance of use. Since it is precisely the ability to cope with genuine discourse that we are aiming to develop in the learner, it would seem on
the face of it that the extract ought to be the preferred kind of reading
passage. There are, however, certain complications. To begin with, the
very fact that these passages are extracted from the context of larger

communicative units and presented in detachment for language learning purposes is bound to reduce their naturalness as discourse. In the normal run of events we do not encounter discourse in the form of separate reading passages but as complete rhetorical units: as essays, articles, letters, newspaper reports and so on. Furthermore, these units are related to the context of our own social and psychological reality. If we read a newspaper report, for example, we do so because we have an interest in its topic and as we read we associate the contents with our existing knowledge. We read what is relevant to our affairs or what appeals to our interests; and what is remote from our particular world we do not bother to read at all. To present someone with a set of extracts and to require him to read them not in order to learn something interesting and relevant about the world but in order to learn something about the language being used is to misrepresent normal language use to some degree. The extracts are, by definition, *genuine* instances of language use, but if the learner is required to deal with them in a way which does not correspond to his normal communicative activities, then they cannot be said to be *authentic* instances of use. Genuineness is a characteristic of the passage itself and is an absolute quality. Authenticity is a characteristic of the relationship between the passage and the reader and it has to do with appropriate response.

One of the difficulties about extracts, then, is that although they are genuine, the fact that they are presented *as* extracts imposed on the learner for language learning purposes necessarily reduces their authenticity. If a learner is to acquire communicative abilities he must ultimately be induced to treat reading passages as discourse, to adopt the same attitude to them as he would to written discourse in his own language. This is not achieved simply by confronting him with genuine instances of language use. We have to resort to pedagogic contrivance. Our problem is this: how can we present reading material in such a way as to persuade the learner to consider it as normal language use, even when it is not. There are a number of possibilities.

In the first place, there seems to be no reason, in principle, why passages should not be linked together to take the form of a normal rhetorical unit. One might take an exchange of correspondence and deal with one letter at a time, or an article and deal with one or two paragraphs at a time. In each case, having introduced the parts of the discourse one by one in sequence one could then consider the whole as a complete unit. Such a procedure might help to authenticate the extracts by restoring them to a rhetorical context. We still have the problem of the more general communicative context, however: the learner may simply not feel himself in any way engaged by the text being presented to him and so may refuse to authenticate it by taking an interest. This means, among other things, that the topic of the discourse has to be one which will appeal to the learner in some way. Here again we might consider the suggestion made earlier that the teaching of language might profitably be associated with other subjects in the school curriculum. If reading passages are combined to form a rhetorical unit dealing with matters relating to these subjects there is a chance that the learner's interest might be engaged and he might be led to recognize the relevance of foreign language study to his other school activities. In this way, the foreign language is represented as having the same kind of communicative function as his own language.

Of course, it might be objected that such an association does not stimulate the learner if he is not interested in the other subjects on the curriculum anyway. It might, indeed, have the opposite effect. This is true. But I think it has to be accepted that language learning is, when induced by formal teaching, a school activity controlled by general pedagogic principles. One argument against linking language learning with other subjects is that a foreign language should be used to transport the learner out of the classroom into the more real and exciting world of wider experience. But it is surely the aim of *all* school subjects to do this: all teachers would subscribe to the view that their subjects should appeal to the interest and extend the experience of learners so as to project their attention beyond the classroom. The purpose of pedagogy is not to deny reality but to develop a heightened awareness of it. So by linking foreign language teaching with other school subjects one draws on the motivational benefits of their methodology.

One way of giving extracts a communicative reality, of setting up conditions favourable to authentication, might, then, be to combine them into a rhetorical whole whose topic relates to other areas of the learner's studies. There are, no doubt, other possibilities which might be explored. One might consider, for example, textualizing the discourse both in the foreign language and in the learner's own mother tongue. Let us suppose that we have a passage consisting of, let us say, ten paragraphs representing a self-contained unit of discourse on some topic which might be expected to engage the learner's attention. We might present the first two or three paragraphs in the mother tongue and then switch to the foreign language for a paragraph. The learner's normal reading strategy is engaged as he reads the first paragraphs, the theme is established and expectations projected forward: he is launched into the reading process. In this way, that part of the passage which is textualized in the foreign language might be conditioned into authenticity.

4.3.2 *Extracts: the comprehending problem*

One of the difficulties, then, of presenting reading passages in the form of extracts is that, though genuine enough, they may not engage the learner's attention in such a way as to render them authentic. He may not be motivated to read something outside the context of his normal concerns, an isolated instance of language imposed upon him for a language learning purpose. Of course, the same objection can be made about simple accounts and simplified versions, which I will consider presently, but there the claim for authenticity is not likely to be made. More of this later. Meanwhile, there is another difficulty about extracts that needs to be mentioned, and which simplified versions and simple accounts are expressly designed to counteract. It is this: even if the learner is motivated to read a particular extract and is ready to give an authentic response, he will be denied the opportunity if the linguistic difficulty of the passage is such that he cannot process it. So far I have been pointing to features of the extract which might make it difficult to read, as discourse; features which do not provide for the kind of conditions in which this communicative ability normally operates. But as was noted in the previous chapter communicative abilities presuppose linguistic skills and part of the ability to read lies in the skill of comprehending. We must clearly take care that passages do not present difficulties of usage which would prevent the learner comprehending to the extent necessary to read the passage effectively as discourse. Clearly a genuine instance of use cannot be authenticated if it consists of syntactic structures and lexical items which the learner just has not the competence to comprehend.

One solution to this dilemma, and one which is quite commonly resorted to, is to provide a list of words and phrases and their meanings for the learners to go through (often as an oral class activity) before they begin to read. The words and phrases in a glossary of this kind are those which are judged to be outside the learner's current competence and which would otherwise, therefore, pose a comprehending problem. We might call explanations which precede the reading passage like this *priming glossaries* since their purpose is to prepare the learner beforehand for his encounter with possible problems in the passage. An alternative procedure, also quite common, is to provide what we might call *prompting glossaries*. These are explanations which are linked to particular problems as the reader actually encounters them in context. They usually appear after the passage and it is assumed that the reader will refer to them whenever he comes up against a difficulty. Occasionally, however, prompting glosses appear as footnotes or in the margins alongside the passage itself.

4.3.2.1 *Priming glossaries*   Let us at this point consider some possible examples of both kinds of glossing procedure and try to establish their function and relative effectiveness. We will assume that we have extracted a passage from a Geography textbook and that we have identified a number of words and phrases which seem on the face of it to be potentially difficult for our learners. We might produce a priming glossary like the following (the entries have been given a letter for ease of reference):

Underground water

(a) approximately—about
(b) remainder—the rest of the water
(c) compacted—packed together*[1]
(d) layer—a thick sheet
(e) porous—allowing liquid to pass through*
(f) penetrates—soaks through
(g) filter—to flow through*
(h) encounters—comes to
(i) impervious—not allowing water to pass through*
(j) seep—to trickle, to flow in drops*
(k) percolates—soaks through
(l) arrested—stopped
(m) collects in the interstices—fills up the gaps
(n) particles—very small bits*
(o) saturated—full of water
(p) breaks—comes
(q) springs—places where there is water coming up from the ground*
(r) as a permanent feature of—always present in
(s) the landscape—that part of the country
(t) emerge—appear

[1]When water falls on the surface of the earth as rain or snow, approximately half of it evaporates. [2]Of the remainder, about half stays on the surface and runs off in streams and the rest soaks into the soil and the loosely compacted upper layer of porous rock. [3]The water which penetrates the surface filters through the soil and rock until it encounters a lower layer of closely compacted impervious rock like clay. [4]This prevents it from seeping further into the ground. [5]So water percolates down through porous material until it is arrested by an impervious layer. [6]It then collects in the interstices between rock particles until these are full and the soil or porous rock becomes saturated. [7]The total volume of a loosely compacted rock like sandstone may, when it is saturated, contain a very high proportion of water. [8]The level at which saturation begins is called the water table.

[9]Water does not only filter directly downwards. [10]It also percolates outwards from the upper parts of the water table. [11]When the water table breaks through the surface, water may come out of the ground in the form of a line of springs along the outer edge. [12]Where a layer of impervious rock appears on the surface at the same place, these springs

may remain as a permanent feature of the landscape. [13]Since water cannot seep down through the rock, it is forced to emerge on the surface.

What kind of observation can we make of this priming glossary? Perhaps the first thing to notice is that the explanations which are provided fall into two categories. Some of them (including all which are marked with an asterisk, *) give the *signification* of the lexical item concerned, its definition as a linguistic element in the language code. Other explanations ((b), (h), (p), for example) provide the *value* which the lexical items take on in this particular context. So some glosses are explanations of usage and some are explanations of use in respect of particular words. Now in the case of signification glosses, the learner has to perform a further operation on the explanation so that it fits into the context. He cannot transfer it directly but must adjust it in some way. This adjustment may be principally syntactic. For example, the learner cannot simply replace the word *porous* in sentence 2 with the gloss given in entry (e) since this would yield the ungrammatical expression:

the loosely compacted upper layer of allowing liquid to pass through rock.

What the learner has to do is to extract the basic meaning from the explanation and apply it appropriately when the word which is glossed appears in the passage. And this may involve him in semantic as well as syntactic adjustment. Consider, for example, entries (g) and (j). The words *filter* and *seep* are given different meanings because it is their signification which is specified. But when the learner encounters them in the actual passage he has to adjust these meanings so that they become synonymous because these two words take on the same value in the context. It is true that if one is specifying the signification of these words, one would wish to make a distinction between them; but the point is that this distinction is neutralized in this particular instance of use. It should also be noted that both of these words are glossed with reference to the word *flow*. In the *Oxford Advanced Learner's Dictionary of Current English* the signification of *flow* is given as: 'move along or over as a river does; move smoothly'. But in the passage, the movement of water downwards is not represented as smooth or river-like at all, but as a gradual absorption. Again, the signification of *flow* has to be adjusted to arrive at the appropriate value.

We might compare the signification glosses (g) and (j) with the value glosses (f) and (k). Both *penetrates* and *percolates* are given the same gloss: 'soaks through'. This can be transferred directly to the context without adjustment (or in the case of *percolates* with slight syntactic adjustment) to yield:

The water which soaks through the surface . . .
So water soaks down through porous material . . .

Now of course these two lexical items have distinct significations but in the context of this particular passage this distinction is neutralized and they take on the same value. And this value is the same as for *filter* and *seep*: all of these terms could be given the value gloss of 'soak through'.

There is, then, a fundamental inconsistency here. If we were to employ signification criteria, then entries (f) and (k) would have to be changed to bring them in line with entries (g) and (j). The four entries might then read:

(f) penetrate—to make a way into or through
(g) filter—to flow through
(j) seep—to flow in drops
(k) percolate—to pass slowly

If we were to employ value criteria, on the other hand, the entries would read as follows:

(f) penetrate ⎫
(g) filter ⎪
(j) seep ⎬ soak through
(k) percolate ⎭

The question arises: which type of glossing procedure is to be preferred? If we decide on the signification type we must accept that we still leave the learner with the problem of working out meanings from context, of adjusting the explanation provided so that it makes appropriate sense. Furthermore, by giving him a meaning in advance we might be inhibiting this process: we might be giving him the impression that reading is simply a matter of recognizing given and fixed meanings as they occur in the passage. But as has already been argued in Chapter 3, reading is not simply a matter of correlating words as they occur in context with their dictionary signification but of creating value by the process of active interpreting. The provision of signification glosses not only leaves the learner to work out particular values unaided but might actually prevent him from recognizing the need to do so. Glosses of this kind may not only be unhelpful but may encourage a mistaken attitude to the reading task. They have a further disadvantage which must be mentioned. Because of the need to be explicit, signification glosses tend to transfer difficulty from semantics to syntax, from the meaning of the individual word to the grammatical structure of the explanation. Entry (q) is a case in point. What we might call the concept of a spring (of water) is easy enough to grasp (and could be represented ostensively by a simple diagram) but the concept tends to be complicated by the very linguistic means which are used to explain it: 'places where there is water coming up from the ground'. Very often, the syntactic complexity of an explanation deflects attention from the basic meaning of the word being explained and defeats its own object. Thus the learner provided with a signification gloss in a priming glossary may well have to carry out two procedures: he must first convert the explanation of a word into a familiar concept and then modify this concept as the context requires in order to arrive at an appropriate value for the word as it is used in the passage.

One might argue, then, that the signification gloss leaves the learner with too much to do: it does not give him enough help but misleads him into thinking that it does. The argument against the value gloss might be that it leaves the learner with too little to do. If the learner is to acquire the communicative ability of reading then he must develop an interpreting strategy whereby he is able to derive meaning from context. If a glossary provides him with the values of different expressions, then it of course deprives him of the opportunity of discovering them for himself in the process of interpreting the passage.

Both types of gloss might, if used with pedagogic discretion, have some utility in particular teaching situations. Most teaching techniques can be useful if one understands the extent of their usefulness. But it is obviously important that the teacher should be quite clear about the different functions that these two types of gloss can fulfil and should take care not to confuse them. The same applies, perhaps with even more force, to the learner.[2] If he assumes that a certain gloss represents signification when it in fact represents value, then he will have problems when he encounters the same word in a different context. He might be led to believe, for example, with reference to entry (p) that *breaks* has the basic meaning of 'comes' and there will be many occasions when he will not be able to reconcile this signification with the meaning required by the context. If, on the other hand, he assumes that a signification gloss represents value, he will have difficulty reconciling this with the meaning required by the context of the passage for which the glossary has been devised. If the learner does not understand just what status the gloss has, it might well create more difficulties than it resolves.

4.3.2.2   *Prompting glossaries*   Let us now turn to what I have called prompting glossaries. A glossary of this kind for the reading passage given above might take something like the following form:

(a) S1   approximately—about
(b) S2   remainder—i.e. the rest of the water, the water that does not evaporate
(c) S2   loosely compacted upper layer of porous rock—porous rock is rock which allows water to pass through it. It is loosely packed, so water can pass through the spaces.

(d) S3   closely compacted impervious rock—impervious rock does not allow water to pass through it. It is tightly packed so there are no spaces for the water to pass through.

(e) S4   water percolates down through—water soaks through

(f) S4   arrested by an impervious layer—stopped by a layer of impervious rock

(g) S5   collects in the interstices between rock particles—fills up the gaps between the small pieces that make up the rock

(h) S5   these—i.e. the interstices

(i) S5   becomes `saturated—when the spaces between the rock particles are completely filled with water the rock or soil is said to be saturated

    etc.

The first point that might be noted about this prompting glossary is that all of the entries are of the value gloss type: the meanings which are given are those which the phrases take on in the particular sentences referred to. In the case of the first entry here, it happens that the signification of the word is not distinct from its value in this context and a number of other cases of convergence of signification and value occur in this passage (and will occur, of course, in all discourse). But these occurrences are not singled out for individual treatment: instead they are dealt with as part of a more general gloss. It is indeed a feature of this kind of glossary that it tends to deal not with individual lexical items but with much larger units of meaning. Furthermore, some of the entries go beyond a simple rephrasing which can replace the expression which is being glossed. We can compare (c), (d) and (i), for example, with (e), (f) and (g). In the case of the latter group of entries, phrases are provided with glosses which constitute alternative, simpler, versions and the learner can replace one with the other and no syntactic or semantic adjustment is necessary. In the case of (c), (d) and (i), however, there is no possibility of replacing the original phrase with the gloss. The glosses here are, indeed, not so much direct translations into simpler language as commentaries which expand upon what is actually said and which present an interpretation of parts of the passage as discourse.

The disadvantage of a prompting glossary of this kind is that it tends to relieve the learner of the essential task of interpreting the discourse for himself. It provides him with the value of expressions which might prove difficult and thereby reduces the effectiveness of the passage as a means of developing a reading strategy. The learner does not have to work out the relationship between the known signification of linguistic elements and the value they have in a particular instance of use; he does not have to wrestle with the problem of code and context correlation which lies at the heart of the interpreting ability. This means that his attention is directed to the understanding of the particular passage to which the glossary refers rather than to the development of an interpreting strategy which can be applied generally to other discourse, when there will be no prompting glossary to assist him.

There are, then, all kinds of problems involved in providing glossaries of the sort we have been discussing. And, of course, the very fact that such glossaries are provided inevitably gives the passages the character of language learning exercises and so reduces the possibility of an authentic response. Essentially, these glossaries are devices for simplifying the passage, as it were by stealth: they protect the integrity of the extract as genuine discourse and simplify at a distance by conditioning the reader, thereby maintaining genuineness at the expense of authenticity. In view of this, one is naturally led to question the assumption that extracts are the best kind of reading passage to present to learners. What, after all, is the disadvantage of simplifying passages directly?

4.3.3   *Simplified versions*

This brings us to the two other kinds of reading passage referred to earlier in the chapter: simplified versions and simple accounts. *Simplified versions* are passages which are derived from genuine instances of discourse by a process of lexical and syntactic substitution. In effect, what they do is to incorporate the glosses we have been considering directly into an original extract to produce a version which is judged to be within the linguistic competence of the learner. Essentially, then, it is a kind of translation from the usage available to the author of the extract to that which is available to the learner. One of the problems of this procedure is that the simplification of usage can often result in a distortion of use. Let us suppose, for example, that we wish to produce a simplified version of the passage on underground water and that the priming glossary indicates what changes have to be made to bring the passage within the scope of the learner's knowledge of usage. The first two items are easily dealt with: *approximately* is rewritten *about* and *remainder* is rewritten *rest of the water*. But what are we to do with the complex noun phrase *the loosely compacted upper layer of porous rock* which contains three candidates for simplification (items (c), (d) and (e) in the priming glossary)? Clearly we have to adjust the syntax to accommodate them. We might try something like:

. . . the rest soaks into the soil and the upper thick sheet of rock which is loosely packed together and allows water to pass through.

But this is a distortion of the original. The use of the definite noun phrase with a defining relative implies that there is another sheet of rock which is *not* loosely packed together and that both sheets of rock have been previously introduced into the discussion. But if this is meant to be a second mention of something previously referred to, then it is not appropriate to use defining relative clauses anyway. Such clauses are normally used to *establish* a reference rather than to *identify* it, identification being usually a function of modifying adjectives in definite noun phrases. Thus the following is normal:

The rest soaks into the soil and *an upper sheet of rock which is loosely packed together . . . The loosely-packed upper sheet . . .*

The following, on the other hand, is not:

The rest soaks into the soil and *a loosely-packed upper sheet of rock . . . The upper sheet of rock which is loosely packed together . . .*

The problem is that the simplification here, in trying to make meanings explicit within a restricted range of usage, alters the relative prominence of the elements in the original proposition and so changes their function. In simplifying usage in this way one is constantly caught up in problems of propositional and illocutionary development (as discussed in Chapter 2) and it becomes almost impossible to avoid distortion. Since one's focus of attention is on lexis and syntax rather than on the discourse they are used to create, the simplified version always tends towards exemplification.

4.3.4 *Simple accounts*

But then, one might ask, what is to prevent us simplifying use rather than usage, concentrating not on linguistic elements as such but on a reformulation of propositional and illocutionary development? If we do this we will produce what I shall call a *simple account*. What distinguishes a simple account from a simplified version is that it represents not an alternative textualization of a given discourse but a different discourse altogether. It is the recasting of information abstracted from some source or other to suit a particular kind of reader. The source may be a single instance of discourse: I may, for example, produce a simple account of Chomsky's *Syntactic Structures* for first year students at the university. There may, on the other hand, be a multiple source of information: I may, for example, provide my students with a simple account of transformational-generative grammar. By this definition, a simplified version uses its source as a script, whereas a simple account uses its source (where one can be specified) as a prompt. By this definition also, a simple account is a genuine instance of discourse, designed to meet a communicative purpose, directed at people playing their roles in a normal social context. A simplified version, on the other hand, is not genuine discourse, it is a contrivance for teaching language.

It will be obvious from what has been said in the previous paragraph that an extract can in fact be a simple account. One might, for example, select passages from popular journalistic descriptions of scientific discoveries, or from school textbooks. Journalistic descriptions are likely to be reformulations of information from a particular discourse source whereas school textbooks are likely to be drawn from knowledge acquired through a variety of different sources. We might, perhaps, express the relationship between the different kinds of reading passage we have been discussing in the following way:

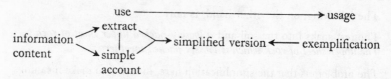

A number of other points might be made about simple accounts as they have been defined here. First, as is indicated in the diagram, simplified versions can be derived from them, as they can from extracts, if this were felt to be necessary. Indeed, our passage on underground water can be considered a simple account, and this did not prevent us attempting to work out a simpler version. Second, the simplicity of accounts is variable and can be adjusted according to requirement. Thus we can have a simple account of a simple account, or several simple accounts of varying degrees of complexity relating to the same area of information content. A third point touches on a theme which recurs as an underlying motif throughout this book. It is that simple accounts are the general stock in trade of other subjects on the school curriculum. All pedagogy involves simplification of this sort in that it aims at expressing propositions and illocutions, concepts, beliefs, attitudes, arguments and so on in such a way as to accord with the knowledge and experience of learners. The methodologies of these subjects are engaged in the production of simple discourse and its gradual elaboration into more complex kinds of communicative use. Language teachers tend to think of grading in terms of usage control: teachers of other subjects are necessarily involved in the grading of language use, in an increasing elaboration of simple accounts.

The points that have been made about simple accounts and the other kinds of reading passage we have distinguished indicate, when taken together, what we have to bear in mind when presenting language data for the development of the reading ability. The language must be such that the learner is willing and able to react to it authentically as an instance of discourse. This means, on the one hand, that passages have to engage the learner's interest and impress him as being in some way relevant to his concerns, and on the other hand be pitched at an appropriate level of linguistic difficulty. The passages should draw upon and extend the learner's knowledge of usage while at the same time developing his knowledge of use, thus deriving reading ability from the comprehending skill.

4.4 Gradual approximation

In view of considerations like these, I should like to suggest that language for reading might be presented by means of a procedure which I shall call *gradual approximation*. This involves the development of a series of simple accounts of increasing complexity by reference to two sources: a linguistic source in the form of a set of sentences, and a non-linguistic source in the form of a diagrammatic representation of information. The sentences provide the usage base and the diagram provides the communicative context. Consider, for example, the passage on underground water. We present the learner with a labelled diagram illustrating the processes described. Notice that such a diagram is an instance of genuine communication, part of the actual discourse of textbook instruction, and not a visual aid to language learning. We also present the learner with a set of sentences which express propositions derived from the diagram, some of which are true and some of which are false. His task is to distinguish the true propositions from the false ones. The following are examples (the diagram labels to which the sentences refer are given on the left):

Vapour—   (a) The water that falls on the earth's surface turns into vapour.
          (b) Some of the water that falls on the earth's surface turns into vapour.
Streams— (c) Some water stays on the surface and becomes streams.
Soil—   (d) Some water goes down into the soil.
Porous Rock—(e) Water goes through porous rock.
          (f) Porous rock is tightly packed.
          (g) Porous rock is loosely packed.
          (h) Water does not soak through porous rock.
Impervious (i) Water does not percolate through impervious rock.
Rock—   (j) Impervious rock is tightly packed.
Interstices—(k) Water collects in the spaces between small pieces of rock.
Saturated— (l) The soil and rock above an impervious layer fill up with water.

The learner is required to bring his comprehending skill to bear on each of these sentences but since they relate to given information in the diagrams he also reads them as statements and can assess whether they are true or false. At the same time, his attention is drawn to the meaning of certain expressions without being subjected to a glossary: thus the equivalence in this context of *go through*, *soak through* and *percolate through* can be deduced, at least as a hypothesis, by associating (e), (h) and (i) and the equivalence of *interstices* and *spaces*, *saturated* and *fill up with water* are suggested by the association of labels and sentences in (k) and (l). Of course the learner cannot be sure of these equivalences: they are suggested in his mind as possibilities. Our knowledge of vocabulary develops from associations of this kind, and by drawing tentative conclusions about meanings by contextual association in this way the learner is already beginning to engage his reading ability.

At the next stage of the proceedings we devise a simple account by combining those sentences which express true propositions. This account will serve as a check on the learner's decisions about the truth and falseness of the statements in the first stage, and confirm his hypotheses about the meanings of certain words. One such simple account might take the following form:

Water in the form of rain and snow falls on the surface of the earth and some of it turns into vapour. About half of it, however, stays on the surface and becomes streams, or soaks into the soil and porous rock near the surface. The water which goes through the surface filters through soil and porous rock until it comes to a layer of impervious rock. This rock stops the water from percolating further into the ground and the water collects in the interstices between rock particles. The soil and rock above the impervious layer become saturated. The level at which saturation begins is called the water table.

The simple account derives from both the set of sentences and the diagram. Increased demands are made on the learner's reading ability: he has to infer propositional links by recognizing the value of certain anaphoric elements (like *it*, *this rock*, etc.) and to realize the value of lexical items by referring to the context and his own knowledge, part of which we have of course provided for in the first stage of the operation. Exercises can be devised to draw the learner's attention to these interpreting activities. I will consider these later when we come to the question of how reading passages might be exploited. For the present we are concerned with presentation.

After this simple account we can provide another, more elaborate one. In the present case, we might now introduce the passage on underground water as it was given earlier in this chapter but perhaps extended into a longer account. I will repeat the first paragraph here for ease of reference:

When water falls on the surface of the earth as rain or snow, approximately half of it evaporates. Of the remainder, about half stays on the surface and runs off in streams and the rest soaks into the soil and the loosely compacted upper layer of porous rock. The water which penetrates the surface filters through the soil and rock until it encounters a lower layer of closely compacted rock, like clay. This prevents it from seeping further into the ground. So water percolates down through porous material until it is arrested by an impervious layer. It then collects in the interstices between rock particles until these are full and the soil or porous rock becomes saturated. The total volume of a loosely compacted rock like sandstone may, when it is saturated, contain a very high proportion of water. The level at which saturation begins is called the water table.

The account then continues through the next paragraph or paragraphs. The assumption is that the preceding stages in the gradual approximation process will have primed the learner to read on. The first simple account through its association with the diagram is set in a relevant communicative context and so should provide the conditions for authenticity; and because of its association with the set of sentences it should not present usage difficulties which might otherwise block the learner's efforts at authentication. The transition to the first paragraph of the second account should be easy and it is assumed that the paragraphs which follow, developing as they do a theme already established, will engage the learner's reading ability already activated by the earlier stages of the process.

This is just an illustration of how gradual approximation might work but it is, I think, flexible enough to allow for adaptation to different learners and to different kinds of discourse. With regard to the former, we can vary the number of sentences given in the first stage, their linguistic complexity, the amount of detail given in the diagram and the degree of dependence of the sentences on it; all of these can be adjusted to suit particular learners. As the name suggests, grading is an integral feature of the process of gradual approximation. With regard to the adaptation to different kinds of discourse, a simple account may be a summary of general ideas in a piece of expository writing and succeeding accounts in the gradual approximation process would then expand this with illustrative examples which the learner himself could be guided to select. Or we might begin with a simple account of historical events related to maps or chronological charts and then introduce causes and consequences in further, expanded, passages. Alternatively, a series of accounts might begin with the abstract of the main points of an argument and go on to their development through substantiation. In all of these cases, gradual approximation involves the controlled projection from a single paragraph to a passage containing several.

4.5   Comprehension questions: forms and functions

Discussion so far in this chapter has centred on the problem of the presentation of language data for reading, on how we might ensure (so far as we can ensure anything) that the learner's reading ability is engaged and not deflected by communicative irrelevance nor blocked by linguistic difficulty. I do not wish to claim that the problem has been anything like solved. My purpose has been to try to clarify the issues involved and to suggest one procedure for presentation which might be worth exploring. But we must now turn from presentation to exploitation. At the beginning of this chapter I mentioned that it was common practice to teach reading through reading passages with appended 'comprehension questions'. We have been discussing reading passages: we must now discuss 'comprehension questions'. As before, I will first examine common practice and then consider how this might be revised or extended.

One of the issues which has been much debated in recent years is the relative merit of different types of comprehension question. Thus, arguments have been put forward for preferring multiple choice questions to wh-questions, or yes/no questions. These types of question have to do with how the learner's understanding is to be demonstrated, what kind of overt response is required of him. We are concerned in this case with what *form* questions should take and so with what form of answer the learner should be expected to provide. But we can also think of questions in relation to what *kind* of understanding the learner is expected to demonstrate and here we are concerned with what *function* they have. Decisions about what form questions should take depend on one's views on how understanding might best be checked. Decisions about what functions questions should have depend on what one thinks constitutes understanding in the first place. To clarify this distinction between the form and the function of questions, let us consider the following simple, if somewhat extreme, example. A teacher of rather eccentric cast of mind has developed, let us suppose, a private theory that it is an important aspect of the ability to read to count the number of times the definite article appears in a reading passage. He might, in this case, devise a question whose function was simply to get the learner to count definite articles. But this function could be fulfilled by casting the question in a number of different forms. For example:

How many definite articles are there in this passage?
Are there 45 definite articles in this passage?
There are 45 definite articles in this passage. (true/false)
In this passage there are
    (a) 40 definite articles.
    (b) 30 definite articles.

(c) 45 definite articles.

(d) No definite articles at all.

What I want to do now is to review the different forms that comprehension questions most commonly assume and point out what I see as their relative merits and disadvantages. I shall then go on to consider function.

4.5.1 *Types of question by reference to form*

Generally speaking, we can identify four types of question with reference to form, namely:

A. Wh-questions

B. Polar questions

C. Truth assessment

D. Multiple choice

We may begin our discussion[3] by first observing that A and B type questions are interrogative in form whereas C and D do not take on the appearance of questions at all. There is a simulation in the case of A and B of a normal social exchange whereby one person puts a question to another who then provides a response. In the case of C and D, on the other hand, the learner is presented with statements whose truth he is required to assess against the knowledge he has derived from the reading passage. The activity required of him is not the (apparently) social one of answering somebody's question but the mental or psychological one of measuring the truth of given propositions against his knowledge, working out which of them represents a correct item of information. We may say, then, that type A and B questions are directed towards an external, social response, whereas C and D type questions are directed towards an internal, mental response. Type A and B questions presuppose a questioner and the response is provided to satisfy his (supposed) need for information. But with C and D type questions there is no questioner: only information to be checked against knowledge.[4]

Since type A and B questions require an overt response, they make demands on the learner's capacity for producing language. In fact, many teachers insist that the learner should speak or compose 'complete' (i.e. self-contained) sentences. What this means is that the response is not an instance of saying or writing because the question and response do not combine to create natural discourse. Consider the following:

Q: Where did spices, silk and carpets come from?

A: Spices, silk and carpets came from the East.

Q: Who was said to rule over the East?

A: Prester John was said to rule over the East.

Q: Was Prester John supposed to be rich?

A: Yes, Prester John was supposed to be rich.

Notice that the forms of the answers here are precisely those which would be appropriate to C and D type questions: that is to say, they represent propositions which might be passed mentally under review to be checked against knowledge. They are odd here because they are represented as normal responses, as overt social and not as covert mental activity.

The teacher no doubt feels free to use these question types to exercise the productive skills because he is aware that such questions are pedagogic devices and not normal requests for information. We are not, in normal circumstances, required to submit ourselves to interrogation after having read something, knowing at the same time that the person putting the questions already knows the answers. To cast comprehension exercises in the form of questions only tends to emphasize the artificiality of the enterprise and so to prevent the learner from adopting the kind of attitude which will encourage the development of the reading ability. It might be difficult for the learner to treat the passage authentically when the questions and answers that follow it are not themselves authentic language behaviour.[5]

The difference between A and B type questions and C and D types has to do, then, with social and mental reality. The former pair suggest a social interaction which does not in fact take place. The point may perhaps be made clearer by comparing type B with type C. On the face of it, there would seem to be no real difference between them; *yes* corresponds to *true* (or a tick) and *no* to *false* (or a cross), so the following would seem to be equivalent, the choice between them a matter of personal fancy:

(B) Was Prester John supposed to be rich?
(C) Prester John was supposed to be rich. (true/false) or (tick/cross)

But if we consider how these two sentences might function as elements in discourse, it becomes apparent that they are not equivalent at all. Thus, B is a bound element in a way that C is not: it is the first part of an exchange initiated by one participant and requiring completion by the other participant in the form of a reply. From the learner's point of view it is as if there is someone, out there as it were, pressing him for an answer. C, on the other hand, is an independent statement which calls for no response and is not attributable to any particular speaking role. It represents a proposition which can be considered in detachment, and so can be understood as the formulation of a thought, an opinion, an item of information which might arise in reading a particular passage. It can be taken as a kind of embodiment of something in the mind, a kind of thinking aloud, the projection of mental activity and not intended as a social act at all.

C and D type questions, then, are context free in that they do not require the learner to take on the role of answerer in a question and answer exchange. In asking a question, as a normal communicative activity, the asker, at the moment of asking, assumes that he has the right to put the question and imposes upon the person to whom the question is directed the obligation to reply. Thus A and B type questions must, in some degree, be an imposition on the learner. C and D type questions do not have this disadvantage. It is interesting to note, in passing, that in questionnaires C and D types are generally preferred to the direct questions of the A and B kind. This presumably is to avoid the problem of imposition, to give the impression that what the person filling in the questionnaire is doing is setting down information to formulate the abstract contents of his mind, simply putting what he knows or what he thinks on record for its own sake. He is given the feeling that he is acting on his own initiative, not being pressed by an importunate individual but providing information of his own free will, to be processed, perhaps, by an impersonal computer. The interpersonal element, necessarily a feature of the direct question, is removed. This does not mean, of course, that what one reveals in a questionnaire might not have personal consequences. And the imposition might be all the more pernicious for being concealed.

To return to the main theme, we might conclude that C and D type questions are to be preferred to A and B type questions on the grounds that they can be understood as representing formulations of propositions in the mind rather than actual utterances and so can be dealt with as mental abstractions. One is not involved in the complications of social context, in the problems of appropriacy and imposition as one is with A and B type questions.

But one is involved in other kinds of problem. I mentioned earlier that teachers frequently used A and B type questions as a means of practising the composing skill, and this shifts the learner's attention away from reading as a communicative ability: his skill in composing the required sentence has no necessary connection with his ability to understand the passage. As a consequence of this, if the learner produces a wrong answer, the teacher cannot know whether this is because the learner's composing skill is not up to the task or whether it is because he has not understood the relevant part of the passage. Or it may be that the learner has not comprehended the sentence used in asking the question. Here we come to a difficulty with Type D questions. Whereas A and B type questions may be distracting because of a focus of attention on the composing skill as a separate activity, D type questions may be distracting because of a focus of attention on the comprehending skill as a separate activity. The learner is presented with a set of sentences and his first task is to comprehend them. If they are to reflect genuine possibilities of misunderstanding, then the difference between them is likely to be slight, and discriminating between them is likely to make considerable demands on the learner's comprehending skill. But this exercise in discrimination is not related to an understanding of the passage, but is imposed on the learner as a separate comprehending task. Indeed, the effect of such an exercise is to distract the learner from his reading of the passage by focussing his attention on the comprehension of the given set of sentences. Of course, the distraction would be less if the correct alternative were obvious so that the distractors (aptly named) could be discounted at once. But then the alternatives serve no purpose and the type D question approximates to the type C.

It is this type, C, which would seem to be the most satisfactory. In the preceding discussion I have suggested that questions should not strive to simulate any kind of normal social interaction because this only serves to emphasize their artificiality, but that they should be directed at making overt what goes on in the mind. This means that what the learner is presented with should be a proposition which might be derived from his reading of the passage, and which therefore has psychological reality. Since we do not run through a paradigm of possible propositions at different points in our reading, the multiple choice type of exercise does not have this psychological reality. It has the further disadvantage of shifting the learner's attention to the practice of the comprehending skill, just as type A and B questions have a way of shifting his attention to the practice of the composing skill. Type C exercises do not have these disadvantages and one might be inclined to adopt them without reservation. There is, however, one difficulty.

In spite of their different shortcomings, the other types of question do involve the learner in problems of one sort or another. The problems may be of the wrong kind, in the sense that they engage his skills in isolation and do not directly relate to the reading ability, but at least they encourage active participation. But questions of the C type seem altogether too easy: all the learner has to do is to say true or false, put a tick or a cross, and even if he does this without thinking at all he has a 50% chance of being right. This suggests that type C questions need to be supplemented in some way. I have said that they can be regarded as the representations of mental constructs derived from a reading of the passage: what we need is some device which will persuade the learner to regard them in this way and which will show him how they derive from his reading. I will be suggesting one possible way of achieving this later on.

I have been arguing that exercises for developing the reading ability should direct the learner to what goes on in his mind, to his mental behaviour, and not require him to provide anything like a natural overt response. The reason for this, put simply, is that we are not normally required to answer questions on what we have read. There is, however, one kind of overt behaviour that does quite naturally arise from reading. If I am presented with a set of written instructions, for example, I am not required to answer questions on them as a check on my understanding but my understanding can be checked against my ability to carry out the instructions. This suggests the possibility of a fifth type of comprehension exercise: one which aims at eliciting a natural *non-verbal* response. It might appear on the face of it that an exercise of this type can only be applied to certain restricted uses of language, like instructions, but in fact it has a much wider area of application.

In the discussion of discourse in Chapter 2 I confined myself to a consideration of how discourse is realized verbally. But (as I suggested in Chapter 3) it is important to recognize that in order to talk, to say something as opposed to simply speaking sentences, we make use of all kinds of paralinguistic resources of communication: 'tone of voice', gesture, facial expression, posture and so on. Paralinguistic phenomena are usually associated in people's minds with spoken discourse. But a good deal of written discourse draws on paralinguistic resources as well. These include formulae, graphs, tables, diagrams, maps, charts and so on. These paralinguistic modes of communicating are intrinsic to the discourse in which they appear and the ability to read such discourse must involve the ability to interpret such devices as well as the verbal material within which they are embedded. Furthermore, the reader has to recognize the relationship betwen these two modes of communicating, the manner in which the information to be conveyed is distributed between them, the manner in which they complement each other to form coherent discourse. It is often the case that verbal and non-verbal elements in a discourse only make sense in relation to each other and we cannot be said to be dealing with such discourse if we confine our attention simply to those elements which are available for processing by the comprehending skill.

An exercise calling for a non-verbal response might be one which required the learner to transfer information from a verbal to a non-verbal mode of communicating. Thus, for example, he might be asked to complete a diagram or a graph on the basis of his understanding of a verbal account. Such an exercise directs the learner to a careful consideration of what is conveyed in the passage and also requires him to make his understanding overt in a natural way: he is not involved in comprehending and composing tasks which distract his attention from the communicative task in hand. Particularly if one associates the teaching of language with other subjects on the school curriculum, as has been proposed, carrying out information transfer in this way is a natural, and indeed a necessary, activity. As I have suggested, learners who are concerned with discourse in which non-verbal modes of communicating are common have to acquire the ability to interpret them with reference to the verbal environment in which they appear. To do so is an integral part of effective reading. A student of economics, for example, has to learn how to interpret graphs and tables, to use them to represent information expressed verbally and to transfer information from them into verbal discourse. Similarly, a pupil learning physics at school has to understand the meaning of symbols and diagrams and be able to formulate verbally expressed information in their terms. So in asking learners to carry out an information transfer exercise we are getting them to perform a familiar task, and this kind of exercise can be seen as something more than just another language learning exercise: the problem to be solved is not simply one which is contrived to teach language but one which makes use of language in a natural way. These non-verbal devices are not just visual aids.

4.5.2 *Types of question by reference to function*

I shall return to information transfer exercises in the following two chapters. Meanwhile we must now turn our attention from the different forms that 'comprehension' questions can take to the kinds of functions they fulfil, to the kind of understanding of the passage that they aim to elicit.

We can distinguish two broad categories of question, and these correspond to the usage/use and skill/ability distinctions that have been discussed in detail in previous chapters. The first of these calls for a demonstration of the learner's comprehending skill and makes appeal to his knowledge of usage. We will call these *usage reference* questions. The second category calls for a demonstration of the learner's reading ability and requires him to infer meanings from context and to treat the reading passage as an instance of discourse and not just as a conglomeration of sentences. We will call these *use inference* questions. These can be further sub-divided in the light of the discussion on the reading ability in Chapter 3. There, it might be recalled, a distinction was made between *assimilation*, the immediate processing of discourse in linear sequence, and *discrimination*, the selective processing whereby the main points are abstracted and relative significance established. We will say, then, that we have the following types of function:

I Usage reference
II Use inference (i) assimilation
                  (ii) discrimination

4.5.2.1 *Usage reference* Usage reference questions are those which require the learner to engage his comprehending skill. They direct his attention to a particular sentence in the passage and he provides a correct answer by noting how the signification of the sentence of the question relates to the signification of the sentence in the passage. He is not called upon to interpret that sentence as having a discourse value at all. Examples of such questions based on the reading passage *Underground Water* given earlier in this chapter would be:

IA (usage reference, wh-question)
(a) What is the level at which saturation begins called?
(b) What happens when the water table breaks through the surface?

To answer these questions, the learner has to comprehend the signification of the interrogative sentence which serves to pose the question (What is *x* called, what happens when *x*) and look for the sentence in the passage which corresponds with it. Corresponding with these interrogative sentences he will find the following declarative sentences which will serve as answers:

(a) The level at which saturation begins is called the water table (S8).
(b) When the water table breaks through the surface, water may come out of the ground in the form of a line of springs along the outer edge (S11).

In actual fact, in these cases, the learner does not even have to understand what the sentences signify: all he needs to do is to recognize their structural relationship. The same is true of the following examples:

IB (usage reference, polar question)
(a) Does water only filter downwards?
(b) Is the level at which saturation begins called the water table?

IC (usage reference, truth assessment)
(a) Water only filters directly downwards (true/false)
(b) The level at which saturation begins is called the water table (true/false)

All the learner is required to do here is to scan the reading passage until he arrives at a sentence which corresponds lexically and syntactically with the sentence given in the question. He will find that S9 in the passage matches IB (a) and IC (a) and S8 matches IB (b) and IC (b). There is no need for him to comprehend the sentences, let alone interpret them as elements in discourse.

Usage reference does not have to be quite as simple and meaningless as this. More taxing questions can be devised which make greater demands on the learner's linguistic skills. Thus we might frame questions like the following:

IA (usage reference, wh-question)
(a) What do we call the level at which saturation begins?
(b) Where do springs form?

These questions can still be answered by reference to particular sentences in the passage (S8 and S11) but the learner has also to refer to his knowledge of usage to recognize that the active structure of the question has the same signification as the passive structure in S8. And in IA (b), too, he cannot simply rely on syntactic and lexical correspondence. He has to comprehend S11 and then compose his answer: he cannot just make a match and copy. So in this case the learner's skills are more fully engaged. But no demands are made on the communicative abilities, as these have been defined in Chapter 3, since the learner is not called upon to consider what value the sentences might have in context. His attention is directed to their signification as separate units of meaning: the rest of the passage might just as well not be there.

Usage reference questions of varying degrees of difficulty can also be asked by means of the multiple choice format. For example:

ID (usage reference, multiple choice)
Water may come out of the ground in the form of a line of springs when
(i) water runs off the surface of the earth in streams.
(ii) the water table breaks through the surface.
(iii) the soil and rock become saturated.

Here, the learner has simply to trace the structure in the passage which corresponds to one of these alternatives. All he is required to do is to recognize that the following two sentences have the same signification:

Water may come out of the ground in the form of a line of springs when the water table breaks through the surface.
When the water table breaks through the surface, water may come out of the ground in the form of a line of springs.

Again, it should be noted, however, that usage reference questions do not need to be so straightforward. They can be made very difficult by accentuating the syntactic and lexical differences between the prompt sentence in the question and the sentence in the passage with which it has to be matched. The point about such questions, then, is not that they are necessarily simple but that they make appeal to the comprehending skill rather than the reading ability: they focus the learner's attention on sentences as self-contained linguistic items and so do not relate to the passage as discourse at all.

4.5.2.2 *Use inference* Use inference questions, on the other hand, focus the learner's attention on the value of sentences rather than on their signification, on the propositions they express and on the illocutionary acts they count as in context. In brief, they are designed to direct the learner to a discovery of how sentences are used in discourse.

As before, this function can be carried out by means of different forms of question, so that we can have IIA, IIB and so on. Let us consider some examples:

IIA (use inference, wh-question)
(a) Why does the soil above an impervious layer of rock become saturated?
(b) When does saturation take place?

To answer the first of these questions, the learner has to consider how sentences 3, 4 and 6 in the passage combine to form a description. He has to recognize that the value of the anaphoric item *it* in S3 and S4 is 'the water which penetrates the surface' (and note that in S4 it could, grammatically, equally well refer to 'a lower layer of impervious rock'). Similarly, a correct value has to be given to *this* in S4 and *these* in S6, and *then* in S6 has to be understood as referring to the state of affairs referred to in S3 and S4. Furthermore, the learner has to recover the correct value for the conjunction *and* in S6 by realizing that it expresses here a relationship of consequence and does not simply mark additional information. To clarify what I mean by this, in the following sentences:

(1) They shot him in the head and killed him.
(2) They tied him up and killed him.

(1) expresses consequence in the conjunction but (2) does not. S6 is of the first type and not the second and if the learner does not recognize this he will not be able to answer the question IIA (a).

Let us now consider IIA (b). First of all, let us notice that the previous question involves relating S3, S4 and S6: it directs the learner's attention to the immediate process of tracing propositional development through these three sentences. It is therefore concerned, we may say, with reading as assimilation. But what about S5? The learner does not need to refer to this to answer IIA (a): it may, indeed, be something of a distraction. What, then, is its function? Let us note, to begin with, that there is an absence of anaphora in this sentence: the noun phrases are indefinite: *water*, not *the water*, *porous material* not *the porous material*, *an impervious layer* and not *the impervious layer*. In consequence there is no definite article which might function (as in S3, for example) to link the sentence with the ones which precede it. This fact suggests that S5 is in some sense aside from the propositional development expressed through S3, S4 and S6 and functions at a different level of generality. This is borne out by the use of the general term *material* (which takes on the value of 'soil and rock' by reference to S3). But now although there is no overt cohesion through anaphora linking S5 with S3 and S4, the term *so* indicates an illocutionary relation and signals that S5 is meant to function as a concluding statement. What it does, in fact, is to summarize what has been said in the preceding sentences and at the same time lends the description an added feature of generality.

Now question IIA (b) differs from question IIA (a) in the same way as S5 differs from S3 and S4: it is pitched at a higher level of generality, and it refers to a 'main point' in the paragraph. That is to say, it is concerned with reading as discrimination. To answer the question appropriately, the learner has to see that the particular description of saturation given in S3, S4 and S6 is summarized and generalized by S5. He has to see how these parts of the discourse combine coherently as illocutionary acts and to discriminate between the particular and general levels of description. Confronted with IIA (b), then, the learner has to infer a generalization from S3, S4 and S6 and associate it with what is expressed in S5. Notice that the learner cannot produce a correct answer simply by copying from S5. Thus, the following answer:

Saturation takes place when water percolates down through porous material until it is arrested by an impervious layer.

suggests that saturation takes place *as* the water percolates rather than *after* the water has percolated. A correct answer must draw on the proposition expressed in S6 but modify it to achieve the right degree of generality. For example:

Saturation takes place when water percolating down through porous material is arrested by an impervious layer and fills up the interstices between rock particles.

The following answer, however, is not pitched at the right level of generality:

Saturation takes place when the water which penetrates the surface and filters through the soil and rock is arrested by a lower layer of closely compacted impervious rock.

Even less appropriate would be an answer like the following:

Saturation takes place when the water which penetrates the surface filters through sandstone until it encounters a lower layer of clay.

The difficulty with these last two, unsatisfactory, answers is that the learner allows interpretation at the assimilation level to intrude. It seems generally to be the case that learners will tend to treat all questions as usage reference first and then, when that tactic fails, to engage interpretation at the assimilation level. The discrimination level is the most difficult to operate on since it involves not only a recognition of how propositions develop through sentences but also, more crucially, what these propositions count as: which of them take on the value of exemplification, qualification, generalization and so on. At the discrimination level the learner has to perceive the illocutionary structure of the discourse.

As was pointed out earlier, the function of use inference questions may be fulfilled by the other forms of questions discussed previously. Here are examples. The reader may wish to consider what is involved in answering them, and how they might be altered to become more effective.

II B (use inference, polar question)
(a) Does water filter through impervious rock?
(b) Is sandstone always saturated?
(c) Is sandstone a porous rock?

IIC (use inference, truth assessment)
(a) Water filters through sandstone.
(b) Water filters through porous rock.
(c) Sandstone is impervious.

IID (use inference, multiple choice)
(a) Saturation occurs when
     (i) water seeps through the soil.
     (ii) water seeps into sandstone above a layer of clay.
     (iii) water seeps into porous material above a layer of impervious rock.

(b) When water seeps into sandstone above a layer of clay,
     (i) springs of water are formed.
     (ii) saturation occurs.
     (iii) porous material above a layer of impervious rock is saturated.

(c) Spring of water may occur when
     (i) soil becomes saturated.
     (ii) the level of saturation reaches the surface.
     (iii) water reaches a layer of impervious rock.

4.6 Other reading exercises[6]

Our discussion of the forms and functions of 'comprehension questions' still leaves us with the problem of learner participation and I will devote the remainder of this chapter to considering how this might be resolved. The problem arose, it will be recalled, when we were trying to assess the relative effectiveness of different forms of question. I suggested that types C and D might be preferred to types A and B on the grounds that they were directed at the psychological activity of learners and did not involve them in unnatural pretence. Of these two, C was then preferred to D in that it did not involve the learner in irrelevant comprehending tasks. There was, however, the difficulty that learners might run through such questions unthinkingly, guessing at answers without troubling to go through the process of either reference or inference. It was suggested that such questions needed to be supplemented in some way.

One way might take the form of the following procedure. We insert type C statements within the reading passage itself so that at certain points in his reading the learner has to pause and check on his interpretation of what he has read. Since truth assessment statements are, as I have argued, best seen as the overt expression of mental constructs deriving from the reading process, it would seem only appropriate that they should appear, not at the end of the passage, when the process is completed, but within the passage as the process is taking place. To do this is to indicate what kind of status such *interpretation checks* are meant to have. Thus, for example, we might insert the following checks between the first and second paragraphs of our passage on underground water. The reader is required to assess whether the statements are true or false by reference to what is said in the first paragraph:

1. About half of the water that falls on the earth filters through the surface.
2. Impervious rock prevents the penetration of water.

Now it is not enough that the learner simply mark these statements true/false or √/×. We want him to know why he does so: we want his tick or cross to be informed by an assessment based on a reasoned consideration of what is said in the passage. We now attempt to activate this kind of consideration by devising explanatory *solutions* for each statement and by requiring that the learner should participate in working them out. The following might serve as solutions for the interpretation checks given above (the numbers in brackets indicate the sentence in the passage to which reference is to be made in completing the statements):

1. About half of the water that falls on the earth . . . (1) The other half, that is to say the . . . (2), *either* stays on the . . . (2) *or* . . . (2) through the soil and porous rock. About half of the water that does not . . . (1) soaks through the . . . (2)

   Therefore, about a *quarter* of the water that falls on the earth . . . (3) through the surface.
2. Closely compacted rock . . . (4) water from . . . (5) further into the ground.

   Therefore, water cannot . . . (3) closely compacted rock.

   That is to say, water cannot penetrate . . . (5) rock.

   Impervious rock . . . (4) water from penetrating further into the ground.

   That is to say, impervious rock prevents the penetration of water.

The aim of solutions of this programmed kind is to get the learner to participate actively in the reasoning process which is required for interpretation to take place. In completing the solution, the learner's attention is drawn to the way different expressions (like *percolate, soak* and *filter* in the present passage) take on equivalent value in context, and how what is said in one part of the passage interrelates with what is said in another part. In the examples given, the focus is on assimilation and on the links between contiguous sentences but it is easy to see that solutions of this kind can also relate to the discrimination level and establish links between widely separated parts of a discourse. In this case they would operate as programmed summaries of the passage.

It is possible to conceive of other exercises which would concentrate on particular aspects of the reasoning process represented in the solutions. One such exercise might be one which provided additional practice in realizing the value of anaphoric elements like personal and relative pronouns (*it* and *this* for example) and general noun phrases (like *the event, this fact,* and so on). A *contextual reference* exercise of this sort might take the following form:

Rewrite the following sentences by replacing the words in italics with expressions from the passage which make their meaning clear.
1. *This* prevents water from soaking further into the ground.
2. When *it* is prevented from seeping further into the ground, *it* collects in the interstices between rock particles.
3. When *these* are full the soil and porous rock become saturated.
etc.

Essentially, what such an exercise does is to decontextualize parts of the passage and convert them into self-contained statements. It is the reverse of the gradual approximation process discussed earlier, in which a simple account is produced by combining self-contained sentences and making them context dependent.

Another kind of exercise might be one which concentrated on synonymous expressions in context. It was pointed out earlier in our discussion of glossaries that in the passage on underground water there are a number of expressions which have the value 'pass slowly through'—*filter, soak, seep, percolate,* and the second solution given above requires the learner to realize this. An exercise in *rephrasing* might be devised to provide further practice in this aspect of the reading ability. For example:

Rewrite the following sentences by replacing the words in italics with expressions from the passage which have the same meaning.
1. Some of the water which falls on the earth *percolates* through the soil and *loosely compacted* rock.

2. *Impervious* rock prevents water from *soaking* further into the ground.
3. When the *level at which saturation begins* breaks through the surface, springs may occur.

The exercises that have been suggested here are intended to get the learner to actively engage his reading ability and to make him aware of his own interpretative procedures. Their purpose is to support and extend psychologically oriented comprehension questions of the truth assessment type. With contextual reference and rephrasing exercises, at least as represented here, the emphasis is on assimilation. We might now go on to consider, briefly, whether supplementary exercises might not be devised which aim more particularly at discrimination.

One such exercise might make use of the multiple choice format. It will be recalled that an objection was raised against multiple choice questions on the grounds that they lacked psychological reality: we do not normally run through a paradigm of possible propositions when we read in order to select the correct one in the context. So multiple choice questions do not seem to have very much psychological validity with respect to assimilation. But discrimination involves filtering the general from the particular, selecting from propositions not on a basis of their truth or falseness but on a basis of their relative significance. In this case, the multiple choice type of question *would* seem to be suitable. We might, for example, recast exercise IID (a) in the following form:

Select the statement which is the most satisfactory summary of the paragraph.
1. Saturation occurs when
    (i) water seeps into sandstone above a layer of clay.
    (ii) water seeps into porous material above a layer of impervious rock.
    (iii) water seeps into sandstone above a layer of impervious rock.
etc.

This could be followed by a solution which pointed out the difference between particular and general statements. For example:

Porous material—e.g. sandstone (S2 and S7)
Impervious rock—e.g. clay (S3)
Saturation occurs when water seeps into porous material above a layer of impervious rock. Sandstone above a layer of clay, *for example*, often becomes saturated.

This might then be followed by an exercise which requires the learner to discriminate between general and particular statements and to combine them as in the example above. But here we anticipate the discussion of the next chapter.

Meanwhile, we must conclude this present one. In it I have tried to examine, from the theoretical point of view outlined in the first part of the book, how written language is commonly presented and exploited. My aim has been to establish as impartially as possible the advantages and limitations of presentation procedures like simplification and the compiling of glossaries and notes and of exploitation through comprehension exercises of different kinds. Once the apparent purposes and hidden assumptions of common practice are made explicit, one can begin to suggest modifications and alternative techniques. This I have tried to do as well, tentatively, in full awareness that any pedagogic proposal must be provisional and subject to actual classroom experiment.

Notes and references

1. Glosses marked with an asterisk in this way are quoted directly from the third edition of:
   A. S. Hornby: *Oxford Advanced Learner's Dictionary of Current English*, Oxford University Press, 1974.
2. It might be held that it does not matter whether the learner knows what he is doing or why he is doing it so long as the teacher knows. Under the influence of behaviourist notions about the nature of language learning, language teaching pedagogy has tended to discourage the learner from inquiring into the rationale which might justify the activities he is asked to perform. He is meant to submit himself like a circus animal to the direction of the trainer and to respond to the stimuli provided without recourse to thought. Indeed, thinking might easily interfere with the mechanical process of habit formation which, for some behaviourists, at least, is the defining feature of language learning. (See Note 3, Chapter 3). I have taken the view throughout this book that the acquisition of abilities requires the learner to assume a more active and responsible role involving, among other things, an awareness of his own learning processes and of the relevance of particular exercises to their development. It is for this reason that I stress, in Chapter 6, the importance of what I call the principle of rational appeal in the teaching of language as communication.
3. In the discussion that follows, the focus of attention is on the kind of linguistic behaviour elicited by these four types of question in relation to the skills and abilities defined in the preceding chapter. I do not consider the relative effectiveness of these question types as testing instruments. For a discussion of what is involved in testing language learning, and for a description of the language learner's activities from the tester's point of view, see:

Alan Davies (ed), *Language Testing Symposium*, Oxford University Press, 1968.

It should be noted that one of the principal difficulties about the questions I am considering here, and indeed most language exercises, is knowing how to design them so that they do not simply *test* the learner's competence but *develop* it. One way of doing this (the way I advocate in this book) is to encourage the learner's own self-awareness, as suggested in Note 2 above.

4. With reference to the distinctions made in Chapter 3, A and B type questions are reciprocal, C and D type are non-reciprocal. Since reading is a non-reciprocal (though necessarily interactive) activity, it would appear on the face of it that the latter types are more appropriate for its development.

5. On the other hand, it could be pointed out that this kind of question is of very common occurrence in the classroom whatever subject is being taught, so that it could be argued that the language teacher's use of it conforms to general pedagogic practice. If language teaching were related to other subjects (as I keep on suggesting in this book) then the use of such questions might be justified as a necessary methodological consequence of such a relationship. Clearly if the need for such a relationship were accepted one would have to look very carefully at the whole question of the general pedagogic uses of language. In this connection see:

J. McH. Sinclair & R. M. Coulthard: *Towards an Analysis of Discourse: The English used by Teachers and Pupils*, Oxford University Press, 1975.

Michael Stubbs: *Language, Schools and Classrooms*, Methuen, 1976.

6. The exercise types briefly described here have been tried out experimentally in the *English in Focus* series, to which further reference will be made in the following chapter.

5 Composing and writing

5.1 Preview

In the preceding chapter, I discussed a number of ways in which instances of written discourse might be presented and exploited to develop the linguistic skill of comprehending and the communicative ability of reading. As was suggested at the end of that chapter, and as the perceptive reader will have realized for himself, some of the procedures that were proposed can also be applied to the development of the 'productive' activities of composing and writing. Indeed, in view of the fact that all of these language activities were, in Chapter 3, shown as being ultimately dependent on the underlying interpreting ability, it would be surprising if this were not the case. In the present chapter I shall be concerned with composing and writing and, as before, I shall begin by considering what might be taken as typical conventional practice and then go on to explore ways of extending it. And, as before, the perceptive reader will note, even where I do not point out, the potential application of the procedures under discussion to the development of the 'receptive' activities dealt with in the last chapter. Having thus dealt with the 'receptive' and 'productive' aspects of interpreting in relative isolation, I shall then, in the last chapter, suggest how they might be developed inter-dependently by means of an integrated methodological scheme.

Although differing in all kinds of ways, one can discern in a large number of language teaching courses a common underlying pattern of presentation. This consists of a sequence of four main sections in each teaching unit: a reading passage, a set of comprehension questions, a set of grammar exercises and some kind of exercise in composition. Practice books, designed to supplement and extend the teaching in the course books, tend to concentrate on different sections of this basic formula and give them special attention. Thus, we find books of comprehension passages, which focus attention on the first two sections (although there may be some token exercises in grammar as well), books of pattern practice, which exploit the third section of the formula, and books of guided composition which focus on the fourth. In Chapter 4 our concern was with the first two sections of the formula. In this chapter, our concern will be with the second two sections, beginning with grammar.

5.2   Types of grammar exercise

Grammar exercises may take a wide range of different forms but it is possible to distinguish three basic types by reference to the kind of structural operation they call for. I will refer to these types as *completion*, *conversion* and *transformation* exercises and will deal with each of them in turn.

A completion exercise is one which requires the learner to insert linguistic elements into a given syntactic framework. We might take the following as a representative example:

Complete the following sentences by filling each gap with a single word.
1. Water will always filter . . . soil and porous rock.
2. Rain and snow fall . . . the surface of the earth.
3. The water that penetrates the soil collects . . . spaces . . . rock particles.
4. The thief was captured . . . the police . . . an empty house.

Such an exercise looks straightforward enough. There are a number of points, however, that I think are worth noting. To begin with, we should be clear what kind of knowledge the learner is being required to demonstrate in completing these sentences. On the face of it, it seems obvious enough that he is required to demonstrate his knowledge of how prepositions are used. But consider the first two sentences: here the syntactic structure alone determines that the gaps must be filled by prepositions. If the learner knows that the verbs *filter* and *fall* are intransitive, then he will know that the following noun phrases have to be represented as prepositional phrases of one sort or another. By reference to syntactic knowledge alone, therefore, he might complete these sentences as follows:

1. Water will always filter under/into/through/over etc. soil and porous rock.
2. Rain and snow fall on/through/inside/beside etc. the surface of the earth.

Not all of these responses will be equally acceptable from the semantic point of view, but if we simply require syntactically correct sentences then we are not really in a position to reject them on these grounds.

If we now turn to the third sentence, we note that here the syntactic structure does not determine the occurrence of prepositions in the same way. The verb *collect* can function either transitively or intransitively and the learner has to work out what the sentence as a whole might mean before deciding whether it makes more sense to take 'collects' as one kind of verb or the other. If he takes it as transitive, he might complete the sentence as follows:

The water that penetrates the soil collects *the* spaces *and* rock particles.

If, on the other hand, he takes it as intransitive, then he might complete the sentence as follows:

The water that penetrates the soil collects *in* spaces *between* rock particles.

Now we will be inclined to prefer the second completion to the first on semantic grounds. The point to note, however, is that both are possible syntactically: unlike sentences 1 and 2, sentence 3 does not restrict the learner to one syntactic choice.

Of course it might be objected that all this is really splitting hairs since it is obvious that what the learner has to do is to fill in the gaps with prepositions. But obvious to whom? It is easy for the teacher to devise an exercise with his own expectations in mind without considering the unexpected alternatives that the learner might come up with. It is obviously desirable that both teacher and learner should be clear as to what the learner has to do to complete the sentences satisfactorily.[1] In the present case, it should be clear whether the learner is meant simply to exercise his syntactic knowledge to produce correct, if not very sensible sentences, or whether he is meant to produce sentences which are both correct *and* sensible: sentences which, in other words, have a high potential for actual use. Exercises of the completion type can vary considerably in difficulty. Where the difficulty is consciously controlled as part of a clear pedagogic procedure, this can give the exercise the advantage of flexibility. But where the difficulty creeps in, in default of careful control, the result is frequently confusion.

I shall return to this question of underlying complications in apparently simple teaching procedures in a moment, but first let me give a brief description of the other types of grammar exercise mentioned at the beginning of the chapter. Conversion and transformation exercises differ from completion exercises in that they call for operations on existing sentences. They differ from each other in that the conversion exercise requires the learner to derive one sentence from another in such a way as to change the latter's signification, whereas the transformation exercise calls for structural change without a corresponding change in signification. A conversion exercise based on the sentences we have been considering might take the following form:

Change the following sentences into the past tense.
1. Water filters through soil and porous rock.
2. Rain and snow fall on the surface of the earth.
3. The water that penetrates the soil collects in spaces between rock particles.
4. The police capture the thief in an empty house.

A favourite exercise of the transformation type is one which calls for passive versions of given active sentences. Of the sentences just presented, only the last two have the kind of structure which can be transformed in this way (the first two being intransitive). An instruction to change these into the passive would yield the following:

3. The water *that the soil is penetrated by* collects in spaces between rock particles.
4. *The thief is captured by the police* in an empty house.

The question we must now consider is what kind of activity the learner is involved in when doing these exercises, what pedagogic implications lie behind the different forms they take. We might note, to begin with, that conversion and transformation exercises seem of their nature to be simpler than completion exercises in two respects. In the first place, the former (at least as exemplified here) only require the learner to apply certain automatic syntactic procedures and do not involve him in decisions as to whether the resultant sentences make good sense or not. In fact, their use potential can alter quite radically, as we shall see, but in respect to usage it is assumed that if the given sentences are acceptable, then their conversions and transformations will be acceptable also. The kind of semantic problems which we noted in connection with completion exercises can be avoided. The second way in which conversion and transformation exercises are simpler has to do with the kind of demand that is made on the learner's syntactic knowledge. In the case of completion, the learner has to fit a linguistic item into a given structure so that it combines correctly with the elements of that structure: to put the matter technically he has to perform a *syntagmatic* operation and if he is not informed what kind of grammatical element is needed this task involves him in the psychological process of *recall*. In the case of conversion and transformation, on the other hand, the learner is required to replace one structure with another, with which it is in some degree equivalent. In other (more technical) words, the operation here is of an essentially *paradigmatic* character. Now if, as is frequently the case, given and resultant sentences have been taught in association with each other in paradigms, so that present and past, active and passive forms are linked in the learner's mind, then this task will involve not so much recall as the easier psychological process of *recognition*.

The observations I have made about these exercise types are based on the particular exemplification of them that I have presented. It could be argued that they can be made more flexible: that completion exercises, for example, can be devised in such a way as to decrease dependence on recall and that conversion and transformation exercises can be modified in ways which avoid reliance on a knowledge of syntactic structure alone. This is doubtless true and later on I will be considering ways in which exercises of these types might be revised. My purpose at the moment, however, is to draw attention to the possible difficulties which underlie these apparently simple and straightforward procedures and to stimulate a more critical appraisal of their effectiveness and scope.

5.3 Exercises in usage and use

One very general limitation on the scope of these exercises needs to be mentioned at this point. To the extent that they aim at providing practice in correct sentence construction they are directed at the development of the composing skill without regard to the part that this skill plays in the writing ability. This is a consequence of a concentration on separate sentences in isolation from a context which would give them the character of instances of use. The point of such exercises is not to get learners to make statements in writing which have some communicative purpose but to get them to manifest their knowledge of the working of the system of the language. They are, in other words, exercises in usage. The question arises as to whether we might not adopt a use orientation and direct exercises of these types towards the development of the writing ability.

5.3.1 *Composing sentences in passages*

Since the limitation to usage is associated with the manipulation of separate sentences, it might be thought that one way of achieving a use orientation would be to present the learner with sentences combined to form passages of continuous prose. Unfortunately, this tactic does not in itself guarantee that the exercises will be any less usage oriented than before. To see why this should be so we have to refer again to the notion of authenticity that was discussed in the previous chapter. There it was pointed out that a piece of language (to use a neutral expression) only becomes an instance of use when it is treated as such, that authenticity is a matter of appropriate response to language as communication. Thus, even if the learner is presented with a passage rather than isolated sentences, this passage is treated as usage if the learner is simply required to practise his composing skill on it. Consider, for example, the following passage:

People consider gold to be in some way a noble metal. This is because they can expose it to the air for long periods of time without it becoming tarnished. Furthermore, it is a useful substance since one can melt it down over and over again without much loss in weight. These character-istics explain why craftsmen use gold to make jewellery.

We can ask a conversion question like the following:

Change the verbs in the passage into the past tense.

Now all that this exercise requires the learner to do is to move from verb form to verb form and change each into the past tense. If he knows how tenses are formed in English he will have no difficulty in doing the exercise and he need pay no attention whatever to what the sentences mean or the manner in which they relate to each other in the expressing of propositional development or the conducting of rational exposition. The fact that the verb forms occur in a passage has no relevance to his task: they might just as well have occurred in isolated sentences. The same point can be made about a transformation exercise like the following:

Change the sentences in the passage into the passive.

In this case, the learner moves from sentence to sentence and makes the necessary structural change to produce:

Gold is considered to be in some way a noble metal. This is because it can be exposed to the air for long periods of time without it becoming tarnished. Furthermore, it is a useful substance since it can be melted down over and over again without much loss in weight. These character-istics explain why gold is used by craftsmen to make jewellery.

As before, the learner needs to know nothing about the communicative operation of the sentences he is composing. His attention is directed to usage; features like the cohesive value of the pronouns and of such expressions as *these characteristics* are ignored. We might note that in some way the passivized version of this passage has a more normal ring to it than the active version from which it was transformed. This, we might conjecture, is because the theme that is treated is more commonly associated with impersonal statements in which the main topic (the nature of gold) is given prominence and the facts dealt with in detachment from individual experience. Thus, we might feel, the second passage con-forms more closely to rhetorical conventions, as these were discussed in Chapter 2, than does the first: it has greater use potential. But these rhetorical implications arising from the use of the passive are not brought to the learner's attention. So although the second version may be regarded as a more satisfactory or more normal instance of use than the first, the learner is blissfully unaware of this when he produces it. As far as he is concerned, engaged only in practising his composing skill, it makes no difference whether he derives a passive version from an active one or the reverse.

5.3.2   *Using the contexts of the reading passage*

What I have called a use orientation is not guaranteed, then, by presenting passages rather than separate sentences. What we need is some way of bringing out the communicative value of sentences as they appear in context. But then, we might note, the reading passage to which these exercises are appended already provides a context, so we might argue there is no need to attempt to create another. The question then arises as to how we can make use of the context that the reading passage itself provides.

It will have been noticed that of the sentences we have been using to illustrate the different types of exercise, the first three derive from the reading passage and the fourth deals with a totally unrelated topic. This inconsistency was intended to reflect what I think is common practice. One generally finds that exercises of this kind begin with sentences that relate to the reading passage and then go on to introduce sentences which have no connection with the reading passage at all or with each other. On the one hand, then, there seems to be an implication that grammar exercises should be contextualized in some way by association with the reading passage, but on the other hand there seems also to be an implication that the real purpose of the passage is simply to provide a useful source of sentences which can be augmented at random by the compiler's own invention. On the one hand, there seems to be some recognition that the composing of sentences ought to be seen as part of a more general language activity and on the other hand it seems to be represented as an independent activity carried out for its own sake.

So we frequently find a certain ambivalence in grammar exercises as they appear in textbooks. Some of the sentences presented for treatment imply that there is a relationship between this section of the basic formula and the preceding two (the reading passage and the comprehension questions) but some of them imply that there is no relationship with what has gone before and that this section is quite independent. This ambivalence results in a number of inconsistencies and oddities. To begin with, it is odd to shift abruptly, in the present case, from the filtering of water through soil and porous rock to the capture of criminals. And although I may have made this fourth sentence particularly fatuous to underline the point to be made, it is generally true that learners are required to process sentences expressing a very odd collection of propositions. This oddity is not, it should be noted, a trivial matter. As has been suggested, exercises of this kind can be framed in such a way as to avoid any appeal to meaning, but even if the learner's attention is directed to meaning, the fact that there is no relationship between the sentences means that each is separate and self-contained as a semantic unit as well as a syntactic unit. Not only do exercises of this kind not develop the learner's ability to process sentences as they combine naturally to form discourse but they actually inhibit such a development by directing the learner's attention to the isolation of the sentences as instances of usage.

It should be noted that this is a highly unnatural way of dealing with language. As was indicated earlier in this chapter, and elsewhere, isolated sentences can be said to carry with them a use potential. But this can only be recognized by reference to a considerable communicative competence in the language. When a native speaker of a language is confronted with a sentence presented in isolation, his tendency will be to provide it with a contextual setting, to call up a set of circumstances which might provide the sentence with a communicative value as an instance of use. Indeed, it is extremely difficult to persuade a native speaker to suspend his normal reaction to language and to get him to look at it as usage: his natural inclination will always be to make sense of it as use.[2] With the learner the situation will usually be the reverse of this, largely, I think, because his natural tendencies are inhibited by the teaching techniques he is subjected to. Thus he will treat the sentences he is given as instances of usage since the way they are presented will encourage him to do so. Not until he has had experience of the language he is learning as use will he be able to recognize use potential; not until he has learned how sentences function in contexts will he be able to provide contexts for sentences in isolation in the manner of the native speaker. What this means is that the exercises we devise should aim at developing natural language behaviour. The presentation of sentences as a random set of separate units not only does not encourage but is likely to actually inhibit this development.

In exercises in which the first few sentences are drawn from a preceding reading passage and the remainder invented at random we have the problem, then, that the apparent integrative effect of the early sentences is at variance with the disintegrative effect of the later sentences. It might appear that an obvious way out of this difficulty is to have *all* of the sentences related to the reading passages. But although this may improve the appearance of integration it does not follow that it will make it a reality. Everything depends on the nature of the relationship between the sentences and the passage. Consider, for example, the completion exercise which was discussed earlier in this chapter. If the learner refers to the passage when doing the first three sentences in this exercise, then it takes on the character of a simple usage reference comprehension exercise of the kind discussed in the preceding chapter. All the learner has to do is to trace where the given syntactic frameworks appear in the passage (*filter . . . soil, fall . . . the surface* etc.) and then simply transfer the preposition from the passage to the exercise sentence. There is no shift from usage at all. The fact that the exercise sentences appear as contextualized parts of the reading passage is of no relevance to the learner's task.

So although we want to relate the exercise material to the reading passage, we obviously want to do it in a meaningful way, in a way which will achieve real integration by getting the learner to compose sentences as an integral part of the development of the writing ability. The question is: how can the exercise types we have been considering be used to this end?

5.4   Preparation exercises

I think it might be useful, in approaching this question, to make a distinction first between *preparation* and *exploitation* exercises. By the former I mean exercises which precede the reading passage and prepare the way for it by getting the learner to participate in the actual writing. Preparation exercises, then, play a part in the presentation of the reading passage itself. A model for exercises of this sort has already been proposed in the preceding chapter. It was suggested there that the conventional priming glossary might be replaced by a process of gradual approximation. This required the learner to first comprehend a set of sentences and then to read a passage which incorporated them. It was represented as an exercise in which comprehension is extended into reading but it is easy to see that it can also be represented as an exercise in which composing is extended into writing. In this case, instead of the learner being presented with sentences both singly and combined into simple accounts, he is asked to produce sentences and simple accounts for himself by performing various completion, conversion and transformation operations.

Let us consider an example. Interest in the subject of underground water might by now be flagging a little so we will move from geography to social history. The following exercises represent stages in the production by gradual approximation of the first paragraph of a passage on the growth of the West European city.[3]

I (Completion)

Put the present tense forms of the following verbs in the sentences below:

extend, begin, identify, last, be, end

1. The modern period of the West European city . . . in the early nineteenth century.
2. The medieval period of the West European city . . . the first phase of development.
3. We can . . . three main phases in the growth of the West European city.
4. The modern period . . . the third phase.
5. The modern period . . . up to the present day.
6. The renaissance period . . . about 1500 and . . . about the beginning of the nineteenth century.
7. The second phase of development . . . the renaissance period.
8. The medieval period . . . from the beginning of the eleventh century to the end of the fifteenth century.

II (Transformation)

Group the following sentences into pairs and combine each pair by making one sentence into a relative clause.

1. The modern period of the West European city begins in the early nineteenth century and lasts up to the present day.
2. The first phase of development in the growth of the West European city is the medieval period.
3. The renaissance period begins about 1500 and ends about the beginning of the nineteenth century.
4. The modern period is the third phase of development.
5. The medieval period extends from the beginning of the eleventh century to the end of the fifteenth century.
6. The second phase of development is the renaissance period.

III (Simple account)

Arrange the sentences you have written in II into a short paragraph beginning: 'We can identify three main phases in the growth of the West European city.' Leave out any unnecessary words.

This sequence of exercises will guide the learner to produce a simple account like the following:

We can identify three main phases in the growth of the West European city. The first is the medieval, which extends from the beginning of the eleventh century to the end of the fifteenth century. The second is the renaissance period, which begins about 1500 and ends about the beginning of the nineteenth century. The modern period, which is the third phase, begins in the early nineteenth century and lasts up to the present day.

These, of course, are not the only exercises which can be used in the gradual approximation process. We might, for example, prefer as an alternative at Stage II an exercise with the following rubric:

II (Transformation)

Group the following sentences into pairs. Then show how the sentences are related by replacing the noun phrase in the second sentence with a pronoun.

Example:

The modern period is the third phase of development.
The modern period of the West European city begins in the early nineteenth century.

= The modern period is the third phase of development. *It/This* begins in the early nineteenth century.

or:

The modern period of the West European city begins in the early nineteenth century. *It/This* is the third phase of development.

Stage III will now yield a simple account of something like the following form:

We can identify three main phases in the growth of the West European city. The first is the medieval. It/This extends from the beginning of the eleventh (century) to the end of the fifteenth century. The second (phase) is the renaissance period. It/This begins about 1500 and ends about the beginning of the nineteenth century. The modern period is the third phase (of development). It/This begins in the early nineteenth century and lasts up to the present day.

What kind of task the learner is required to do can obviously be adjusted to accord with his competence in the language. If necessary more exercises can be included to increase the gradualness of the approximation. It may indeed be judged necessary in some circumstances to prepare the ground for what is represented as Stage I by pre-sentence exercises. One way of doing this is to begin the gradual approximation process by introducing a non-verbal representation of information and by developing composing and writing exercises by reference to it. In the present case, such a representation might take the following form:

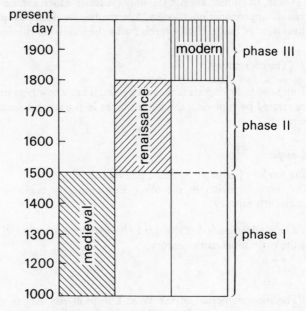

The first stage here might be to get the learner to produce a set of notes along the following lines:

Phase I—medieval period—11th→15th century
Phase II—renaissance period—16th→18th century
Phase III—modern period—19th century→present

Subsequent stages might then consist of completion exercises which lead the learner from the production of simple sentences like:

The first phase is the medieval period.
The first phase begins at the beginning of the eleventh century.
The medieval period begins at the the beginning of the eleventh century.
etc.

to more complicated sentences like:

The first phase begins at the beginning of the eleventh century and ends at the end of the fifteenth century.
The first phase extends from the beginning of the eleventh century to the end of the fifteenth century.
etc.

and then on to transformation exercises of the kind already discussed to yield:

The first phase is the medieval period, which extends from the beginning of the eleventh century to the end of the fifteenth century.
etc.

Non-verbal representations of the kind given above were discussed in the preceding chapter in connection with the process of information transfer, which was proposed as a means of developing the reading ability. There the transfer of information was from the verbal to the non-verbal mode of communicating. Here the transfer is reversed and is from the non-verbal to the verbal. Thus, the same type of exercise can be used to develop both the productive and the receptive aspects of the interpreting ability.

In general, the advantage of preparatory grammar exercises organized into a gradual approximation sequence is that they provide controlled and purposeful practice in composing and writing by getting the learner to participate in the actual compiling of a reading passage. They therefore serve the priming purpose discussed in the preceding chapter: they prepare him for his encounter with a reading passage which can be more elaborate than the version he has produced for himself. In the present case, the first paragraph of such a passage might read as follows:

The Growth of the West European City
It is difficult to be completely accurate about the facts of urban development but we can trace three main phases in the growth of the West European city. The first of these is the medieval phase, which extends from the beginning of the eleventh century to about the end of the fifteenth century. The second is the Renaissance and Baroque phase. This lasts from about 1500 to the beginning of the nineteenth century. The third phase is the modern phase, extending from the early part of the nineteenth century to the present day.

5.5   Exploitation exercises

This brief demonstration is perhaps sufficient to indicate the possibilities of preparation exercises. We now turn our attention to what I have called exploitation exercises. These are exercises which follow the reading passage and exploit it in some way for the provision of practice material. What we require of such exercises is that they should capitalize in some way on the contextualization provided in the reading passage, and use the passage as a basis for the development of the writing ability.

One of the objections levelled against the exercises considered earlier was that they focus attention too exclusively on separate sentences and so only provide practice in the composing skill. But as we have seen with the preparatory exercises just considered it is perfectly possible to associate the practice of a particular aspect of grammar with the writing of simple instances of discourse by gradual approximation. We can provide a similar use orientation for grammar exercises by proceeding in the same way for exploitation exercises. In this case, however, the end product is not a simple version of part of the reading passage but an instance of use which is in some way rhetorically related to it. It may, for example, be a summary of the passage, or a continuation of it, or another passage which exhibits a similar pattern of discourse development.

5.5.1   *Gradual approximation: sentence to discourse units*

Let us, for an example, suppose that the learner has been presented with a reading passage which consists of the description of simple experiments in physics and that this description makes extensive use of the passive (as descriptions of this kind typically do). An exploitation exercise might be devised which provided practice in this aspect of usage while at the same time leading the learner to a description which corresponded to that given in the reading passage. For example:

I (Transformation)

Change the following sentences into the passive:

1. We screw the top on the can.
2. We hold the can under a stream of cold water.
3. Steam fills the can.
4. We boil a little water in a tin can.
5. We remove the can from the flame.

II (Completion)

Refer to the passive sentences you have written and complete the following description:

A little water . . . in a tin can until the can . . . The can . . . then . . . from the flame and the top . . . Then the can . . . from a tap.

Stage I of this operation requires the learner to use his composing skill in transforming sentences (and he will have to be wary of the third sentence). But this is not done in isolation, but as a preparation for the next stage in which he has to complete a short passage, which he can accept as an instance of use to the extent that it parallels the descriptions of experiments already presented in the reading passage. We can increase the authenticity further by providing a set of illustrations of the experiment being described and we can increase the difficulty of the task by asking the learner to write a simple account by direct reference to these illustrations without the help of the framework given in II, or with only the kind of guidance provided by the following rubric:

II (Simple account)

Refer to the diagrams and arrange the passive sentences you have written into a short description.
Combine two sentences with *until* and two with *after*.
Begin the last statement of the description with *Then* . . .

The learner is thus guided towards the following simple account:

A little water is boiled in a tin can until the can is filled with steam. After the can is removed from the flame the top is screwed on. Then the can is held under a stream of cold water.

This is, of course, a short and simple description, but it is easy to see how the controlled introduction of more language work could result in the development of more elaborate versions. And it is easy to see how the procedure can be regulated at different degrees of difficulty to correspond with the competence of different learners. The following, for example, is pitched at a more demanding level of difficulty than the exercises we have just been considering:[4]

I (Transformation)

Change the following sentences into the passive:

1. If we place a smooth roller on an inclined plane, it will run down the plane.
2. Two other forces act on the roller.
3. We can apply this force in any direction providing one component acts up the plane.
4. We call the third force the normal reaction—R.
5. We can therefore draw a triangle of forces for the system.
6. The diagram shows this force—P—acting parallel to the plane. (In the diagram, this force . . .)
7. To keep the roller in equilibrium we must apply a force to it. (A force . . .)
8. One is the force due to gravity—F_g—which we can consider to act vertically downwards through the midpoint of the roller.
9. We now find that we have an example of a three-force system. (It . . . now . . . that we . . .)
10. As we assume the roller and plane to be absolutely smooth, this reaction is at right angles to the surface of the plane.

II (Simple account)

Draw the following diagram and label the forces P, R and F_g on it. Then rearrange the passive sentences so that they make a logical paragraph of which your diagram is the illustration. Sentence 1 is already in the correct position.

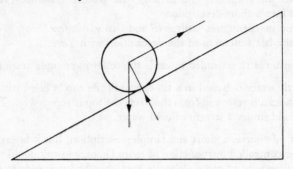

Notice again how the non-verbal representation here serves to relate the productive and receptive abilities. The learner is required not only to combine the sentences he has written into a cohesive and coherent whole (on the model we will assume of what has already been presented in the preceding reading passage) but he has also to label the diagram by reference to the passage he has produced, this production itself being in some degree guided by the diagram. The result is an instance of discourse with both verbal and non-verbal elements such as is commonly found in textbooks of physics and which the learner will therefore be able to realize as authentic language use.

5.5.2   *Gradual approximation: act to discourse units*
In the exploitation exercises considered so far the composed sentences only take on value as use when they are combined to form an account which has the character of discourse in that it has a real communicative purpose. I want now to explore an alternative approach. Instead of beginning with the composition of sentences which are subsequently contextualized in a passage we might begin by focussing attention on different kinds of illocutionary act which can be realized by separate sentences and then go on to introduce ways in which these single acts can be realized over several sentences and can be combined to form larger rhetorical units. Whereas in the approach we have just been considering the learner works up to discourse through the composing of sentences, in the approach now being proposed he works up to discourse through the writing of illocutionary acts.

5.5.2.1   *Focus on single illocutionary acts*   To illustrate what I have in mind, let us suppose that we wish to devise a set of exercises in association with reading passages dealing with topics in general science and that we wish to develop in the learner the ability to use English sentences to perform the illocutionary acts of generic statement, general

statement and definition. Our task is to get the learner to realize that in producing a piece of language like, say:

Aluminium is a gas.

he is not, in the context of scientific communication, simply composing a sentence which can be assessed for grammatical correctness but is also making a statement which can be assessed for its factual validity. We have to woo him away from simple language games and get him to accept the responsibilities of actual communication.

Our first step might be to present an elementary semantic problem like the following:

I

Complete the following diagrams by putting the words in the appropriate boxes.

Lead, nitrogen, nitric acid, copper, thermometer, propane, alcohol, micrometer

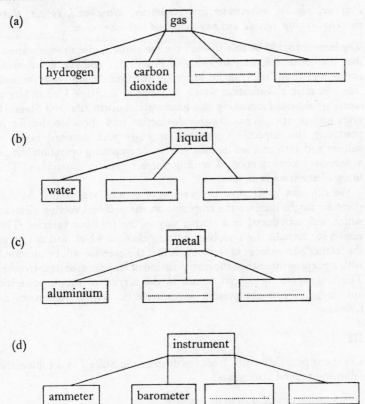

The learner completes these simple diagrams by referring to his own knowledge of science or to a dictionary. The diagrams then form the basis for the next step, which is to get the learner to produce generic statements. This step might be formulated as follows:

II

Look at these statements:

Aluminium is a metal. Water is a liquid. Hydrogen is a gas
BUT: *An* ammeter is an instrument.
Ammeter*s* *are* instruments.
An ammeter and *a* barometer are instruments.
Ammeters and barometers are instruments.
Aluminium and copper are metals.

Now make statements of a similar kind about the following:

Propane, alcohol, micrometer and barometer, nitric acid, copper, thermometer, carbon dioxide and nitrogen, lead and aluminium.

The learner should be able to work out for himself, given the examples, that the terms referring to kinds of liquid, gas and metal are mass nouns and those referring to kinds of instruments are count nouns. The semantic classification which is provided in Stage I gives him a meaningful basis for making this grammatical distinction and Stage II gives him practice in putting this distinction into operation. But he is practising this aspect of grammar, together with concord between subject and verb, not for its own sake as a composing operation but as a necessary consequence of writing correct generic statements. The focus of attention is on use.

We can now proceed to the writing of general statements. At this point we might increase the emphasis on the problem solving element which was introduced in a simple way in the previous exercise. The reason for introducing a problem solving element which will call upon the learner's knowledge of the topic is that the exercise will be provided with a purpose other than the manipulation of language for its own sake. The language is being put to use in the service of simple scientific knowledge. We might present an exercise on general statements as follows:

III

Use the appropriate terms from the diagrams in Stage I to complete the following general statements:

(a) . . . measures atmospheric pressure.

(b) . . . is less dense than air.
(c) . . . burns at a very high temperature.
(d) . . . measures electric current.
(e) . . . is prepared by electrolysis.
(f) . . . is used in thermometers.
(g) . . . contains hydrogen.
(h) . . . has a high relative density.

This exercise takes the form of a completion exercise of the kind we discussed earlier in this chapter but, again, it should be stressed that it is not only the composing skill that is brought into play here. What the learner produces is not just a set of correct sentences but a set of general scientific statements. As a sentence, for example, the following is perfectly correct:

A barometer measures electric current.

But as a scientific statement it is quite wrong.

The exercise on general statements is an extension of the exercise on generic statements carried out by means of completion. In the next stage we can draw on both of these exercises and make use of the transformation procedure discussed earlier in this chapter. For example:

IV

Write definitions by combining the statements you have written in Stage III with those statements you have written in Stage II which are appropriate. For example:

A barometer is an instrument ⎱ A barometer is an instru-
A barometer measures atmospheric pressure ⎰ ment *which* measures atmospheric pressure.

Barometers are instruments ⎱ Barometers are instru-
Barometers measure atmospheric pressure ⎰ ments *which* measure atmospheric pressure.

Although, as before, this exercise provides composing practice, its main purpose is to demonstrate how two communicative acts can combine to form a third: it is concerned with what we might call rhetorical transformation and whatever grammatical transformations are required in carrying out this writing task are dealt with as a means to this end, and not as an end in themselves. Rhetorical transformations, then, change one act into another. This change involves grammatical change also in one way or another and this may be brought about by grammatical transformation, as in the case of the exercise we have just considered, or by what was referred to earlier as grammatical conversion.

It will be remembered that the distinction between these two operations was that whereas conversion involved an alteration of the propositions expressed by sentences transformation did not involve such an alteration but simply replaced one surface form with another. This distinction is no longer relevant in respect to the change in communicative value. Both transformation and conversion in the grammatical sense have the effect of altering the illocutionary act. In the case of exercise IV above, for example, the definition expresses the same proposition as the generic and general statements to which it relates but it is a different act. We can also conceive of a grammatical conversion exercise which would effect an illocutionary change. For our present purposes, for example, we could ask learners to convert general statements into definitions as follows:

V

Change the following general statements into definitions.

(a) Thermometers measure temperature.
(b) Copper is a good conductor of electricity.
(c) A micrometer is used for measuring small dimensions.
(d) Lead resists radiation.

Although grammatically this is a conversion exercise we can recognize that its illocutionary function is of the same sort as the grammatical transformation exercise just considered: both change one act into another. We can refer to both, therefore, as rhetorical transformation exercises.

The kind of approach that has been illustrated here can be used to introduce a wide range of illocutionary acts realized by single sentences. It is worth pointing out that while the particular aim of such exercises is to develop the writing ability in respect of certain acts, they also have the more general aim of making the learner aware of the communicative potential of the language he is learning and of providing him with an orientation to language study which will be favourable to his dealing with the language as a means of communication comparable to his own language. The general purpose of such exercises is to shift the learner's focus of attention.

5·5.2.2   *Relationships between pairs of acts*   Having introduced illocutionary acts as realized through single sentences we have now to apply our principle of gradual approximation to show how such acts can combine to form instances of discourse. As the next move in this direction we might first show the relationships which obtain between pairs of acts. For the purpose of illustration let us consider three such relationships: consequence, qualification and exemplification. The first of these is illustrated by the following pair:

Propane burns at a very high temperature. It is particularly useful, therefore, for welding operations.

The second of these statements expresses a consequence which follows from the truth of the generality expressed in the first statement. This relationship is marked by *therefore*.

The relationship of qualification may be illustrated by the following pair of statements:

Lead has a high relative density. Its melting point, however, is very low.

The second of these statements expresses a qualification which corrects any false impression which might have arisen from the first statement. The marker of communicative function which indicates the relationship here is *however*.

The relationship of exemplification may be illustrated by the following pair of statements:

Some metals have a very low melting point. Tin, for example, melts at a temperature of 232° C.

The marker of communicative function *for example* itself provides sufficient explanation as to the nature of the relationship here.

I have spoken of these relationships as holding between pairs of statements each realized by a separate sentence but it should also be noted that those which I have referred to as consequence and qualification can be expressed also within one statement realized by complex sentences. Thus the relationship of consequence illustrated above by two statements linked with the marker *therefore* can also be expressed as follows:

Since propane burns at a very high temperature, it is particularly useful for welding operations.
Propane is particularly useful for welding operations because it burns at a very high temperature.

Similarly, the relationship that I have called qualification can also be expressed within a single statement:

Although lead has a high relative density, its melting point is very low.
Lead has a high relative density but its melting point is very low.

These facts suggest that we might devise a rhetorical transformation exercise which presents pairs of statements and requires the learner to transform them into a single statement on the one hand and a pair of related statements on the other. An example of such an exercise might be as follows:[5]

I

Arrange the following statements into pairs and then show how each statement in the pair is connected to the other by using either *however* or *therefore*.

For example:

13 + 1 : High-speed steels retain their cutting edge at high temperatures. They are *therefore* used in the manufacture of cutting tools.

1. They are used for the manufacture of cutting tools.
2. In salt water, serious corrosion occurs.
3. Manganese steel is very hard.
4. It is frequently used for armour plate.
5. They are added to steels.
6. Stainless steels require little maintenance and have a high strength.
7. When it is used to coat other metal, the coating is very thin.
8. Tin resists corrosion.
9. Nylon is tough and has a low coefficient of friction.
10. Bronze has a low coefficient of friction.
11. Chromium resists corrosion.
12. It is added to steels to make them rust proof.
13. High-speed steels retain their cutting edge at high temperatures.
14. Under normal conditions, aluminium resists corrosion.
15. It is used to make bearings.
16. It is used to make fibres and gears.
17. It is used to coat other metals to protect them.
18. Tin is expensive.
19. They are expensive and difficult to machine at high speeds.
20. Nickel, cobalt and chromium improve the properties of metals.

II

Combine the pairs of statements in I into single statements by using either *because/since* or *but/although*.

For example:

1 + 13 : High-speed steels are used in the manufacture of cutting tools *because* they retain their cutting edge at high temperatures. *Since* high-speed steels retain their cutting edge at high temperatures, they are used in the manufacture of cutting tools.

As before, there is a considerable problem solving element in this exercise. The pairings of statements in Stage I cannot be done simply on the basis of a knowledge of English usage: this is what makes it a writing and not just a composing operation. A pairing like 8 + 15, for example will, in Stage II, yield the perfectly correct sentences:

Tin is used to make bearings because it resists corrosion.
Since tin resists corrosion, it is used to make bearings.

But as *statements* these would have little value for an engineer. By the same token, 8 could be combined with 15 to form an instance of text:

Tin resists corrosion. It is, therefore, used to make bearings.
Tin resists corrosion. It is, however, used to make bearings.
Tin is used to make bearings. It therefore resists corrosion.
Tin is used to make bearings. However, it resists corrosion.

The use of pronouns here imposes cohesion on the pairs of statements and so combines them to form a text, but as instances of discourse in the field of engineering they are not well-formed. An engineer would find them incoherent. This is because the propositions expressed in the second sentence of each pair cannot be used to perform the rhetorical acts signalled by the markers *therefore* and *however*.

It follows from this that the ability to write coherent statements of consequence, qualification and so on depends crucially on knowledge of something more than language. Realizing linguistic knowledge as use, as opposed to simply manifesting it as usage, must necessarily commit the learner to an acceptance of conditions which control normal communication. Thus he will have to be concerned not simply with whether his sentence is correct or not but whether the statement that it counts as is true or not.[6] And this truth is only assessable, obviously, by reference to knowledge of the world, and in the present case this knowledge has to do with the characteristics of different metals and their use. The point has been made several times in this book (and it will do no harm to repeat it again here) that if we are to teach use then we must accept that language has to be associated with areas of knowledge and experience which are familiar to the learner and which he will recognize as relevant to his concerns. Use cannot by definition be learned in detachment from the communicative context created by such an association. This means, of course, that the *particular* exercises we have been discussing will be no good at all for those learners for whom the topic is neither familiar nor relevant. Not seeing the communicative point, such learners will simply compose sentences. As exercise *types*, however, they can accommodate whatever topics might be appropriate for particular groups of learners.

But we must return now to the main theme and consider the third relationship that was mentioned: that of exemplification. Here we may proceed in much the same way as before by first getting learners to sort out pairs of statements from a randomly ordered set and then requiring them to link up each pair by using the marker *for example*. We might present a set of statements like the following:

1. Magnetic force is concentrated near the poles of a magnet.
2. All substances, except those which decompose when heated, can be changed from one state into another.
3. If a bar magnet is placed in iron filings, most of the filings adhere to the ends.
4. Ice can be changed into water and water can be changed into vapour.
5. If a point, A, is twice as far below the surface as another point, B, then the pressure at A will be twice as great as the pressure at B.
6. Like poles repel and unlike poles attract each other.
7. Metals expand when heated.
8. Pressure in liquids depends on depth.

A variation on the previous format has been introduced into this exercise: not all of the statements given do, in fact, link up to form pairs which can be associated by *for example*. In the course of his sorting and ordering, the learner has to reject statements 6 and 7. Again, it should be noted that there is nothing objectionable about the sentences nor about the text they form in the following cases:

All substances, except those which decompose when heated, can be changed from one state into another. Metals, for example, expand when heated.

Magnetic force is concentrated near the poles of a magnet. Like poles, for example, repel and unlike poles attract each other.

The difficulty with these combinations is not that they are linguistically incorrect, nor that they do not constitute text, but that they lack coherence and so do not make much sense as discourse.

5.5.2.3 *Extension to larger discourse units* Sufficient illustration has now, perhaps, been given of how we might move from a consideration of different illocutionary acts as single statements to a consideration of ways in which acts can combine to form minimal units of discourse, in which two acts can be coherently linked to form a rhetorical sequence. The next stage in gradual approximation is to create larger discourse units building up to the paragraph. Let us see how we do this by reference to the exercise on exemplification. Consider the following statements:

Pressure in liquids depends on depth. (Statement 8)
The pressure exerted at different points will vary according to how far they lie beneath the surface.
The pressure will increase proportionately in relation to depth.
If a point, A, is twice as far below the surface as another point, B, then the pressure at A will be twice as great as the pressure at B. (Statement 5)

The relationship between the first and the fourth of these statements (between 8 and 5) was previously established as one of exemplification. But what is the function of the second and third statements here, and if we now proceed to relate them with the others, does the previous relationship of exemplification still hold? The second of the statements given above is really a restatement of the first: it repeats the proposition of the first in more simple or more explicit terms. We might give such a function the name of clarification and it can be made more explicit by such markers as *that is to say* or *in other words*. The third statement fulfils rather a different function: it provides us with the additional information that the variation in pressure is proportionate to increase in depth. So this statement is an elaboration or extension of what has been said before and here the appropriate markers are *furthermore* or *moreover*. We are now in a position to specify a four act sequence of the following sort:

generalization + clarification + elaboration + exemplification.

This formula will enable us to combine the statements given above in the following way:

Pressure in liquids depends on depth. That is to say, the pressure exerted at different points will vary according to how far they lie beneath the surface. Furthermore, the pressure will increase proportionately in relation to depth. If, for example, a point, A, is twice as far below the surface as another point, B, then the pressure at A will be twice as great as the pressure at B.

We must notice, however, that the exemplification is now related not to the generalization but to the elaboration. On the other hand, the elaboration relates to the generalization through the preceding clarification, this being, as it were, an optional element. This indicates that the discourse we are developing here cannot satisfactorily be represented simply as a linear sequence of acts, each having equal status. We need some kind of hierarchical arrangement which shows that the link between the generalization and the elaboration represents the main propositional development, or theme, whereas the other acts play a supporting role. Instead of a linear representation, therefore, we need a hierarchical one of the following kind:

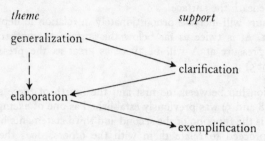

Let us now consider three more statements, and see how we might incorporate them into our sample discourse:

If a point, A, is further below the surface than another point, B, then the pressure at A will be greater than the pressure at B.
The pressure exerted by solid objects depends on the area of contact.
The smaller the area of contact is, the greater will be the pressure exerted.

The first of these statements could function quite appropriately as an exemplification of the existing generalization. The second of them introduces new information: it takes the form of another generalization which refers to pressure in relation to solid objects as opposed to liquids. The third statement is an elaboration of this second generalization. We can now extend our formula as follows:

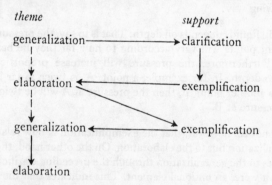

This will yield the following instance of discourse:

Pressure in liquids depends on depth. That is to say, the pressure exerted at different points will vary according to how far they lie beneath the surface. If, for example, a point, A, is further below the surface than another point, B, then the pressure at A will be greater than the pressure at B. Furthermore, the pressure will increase proportionately in relation to depth. If, for example, a point, A, is twice as far below the surface as another point, B, then the pressure exerted at A will be twice as great as the pressure at B. The pressure exerted by solid objects, on the other hand, depends on the area of contact. The smaller the area of contact is, the greater will be the pressure exerted.

There are two points to be noted about this piece of discourse. The first is that the last statement in it, which functions as an elaboration, is not explicitly marked as such by the use of *furthermore* or *moreover*. The reason for this seems to lie in the fact that there is a further condition on the use of markers of this sort, which has to do with how much supporting material intervenes between the generalization and the elaboration which relates to it. If there is none, as in the present case (the arrow here is a continuous and not a dotted one), these markers tend to be omitted since the relationship is clear without them. The use of such markers seems to be a signal to the return to the main theme, so that if there has been no departure from the main theme there is no need for the signal.

The second point to note is that the second generalization is marked by the expression *on the other hand*, which makes explicit the relationship of contrast with the first. If they contrast, however, then they must do so by virtue of the fact that they both relate to a common theme, in this case the concept of pressure. The more intervening support acts there are between the main theme acts which are to be related (i.e. the longer the dotted lines), the more difficult it is to establish this relationship. One might say that the reader assumes up to the point of the appearance of the second generalization that there is only one theme, that which is represented by the opening generalization. It is for this reason that the second generalization is likely to be the beginning of a new paragraph, the main function of the paragraph being to reinstate the main line of argument. The paragraph can be defined as a device of signalling a return to the main theme. Alternatively, we might retain the second generalization in the same paragraph, but then we need to indicate that the theme of this paragraph is a more general one which associates the two generalizations by the relationship of contrast. We can do this by introducing a statement at the beginning or by providing the paragraph with a heading like *The Measurement of Pressure*. Such a heading delineates the scope of the paragraph and prepares the reader for the contrast between generalizations, thus allowing for the possibility of more support acts to be used without distracting attention from the main theme.

We can, then, represent our sample piece of discourse either as one paragraph or as two according to the following formulae.

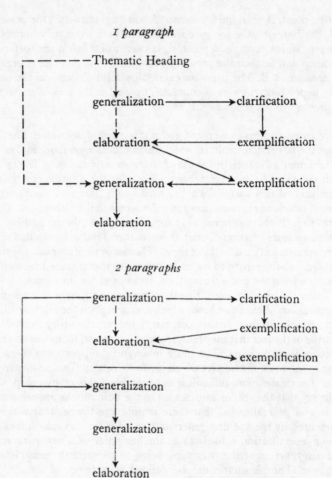

1 paragraph

2 paragraphs

If one adopts the two paragraph version, the first generalization needs to be restated so that its relationship to the second is made clear. This can be done by using the restatement marker *then*, so that the second paragraph would begin:

Pressure in liquids, then, depends on depth. The pressure exerted by solid objects, on the other hand, depends on area of contact.

What I have demonstrated here, in brief, is how one might proceed by gradual approximation to build up discourse units, beginning with pairs of acts, going on to series of acts in linear sequence and then on to the hierarchical arrangements which constitute paragraphs. The sequence of writing exercises need not follow this progression. Instead of moving from pairs of acts to longer sequences, as we have done here, one might begin with main theme acts and then gradually introduce support acts to fill them out into paragraph units. Thus, one might begin with the following:

Whereas pressure in liquids depends on depth, the pressure exerted by solid objects depends on area of contact.

This can be reformulated into a pair of related statements by means of the marker *on the other hand.*

Pressure in liquids depends on depth. The pressure exerted by solid objects, on the other hand, depends on area of contact.

Various statements can now be presented and the task of the learner is to insert them as support acts between the theme acts given above, gradually extending the discourse up to the point when a paragraph division becomes necessary, or, if a more general theme statement is given, until the paragraph is complete in relation to that theme.

The process of gradual approximation from exercises dealing with single acts of communication to those dealing with larger units of discourse has, of course, to be carefully controlled and in this respect the familiar principles of grading associated with the 'structural' approach to teaching apply also to the 'communicative' approach that is being proposed here. The principles are more difficult to apply to illocutionary acts and their function in discourse development because we know much less about paragraphs than about sentences and because there is no authoritative description to which the teacher can refer. There is no pedagogic account of English use comparable with the many accounts of usage now available. In time one might hope that this lack will be remedied.[7] Meanwhile, however, there is much that the practising teacher can do for himself. Although it would be wrong to minimize the difficulties, a great deal of progress can be made towards the design of teaching materials for developing the writing ability, once the teacher accepts the need for a communicative orientation to his task.

I have spoken of these exercises in gradual approximation as developing the writing ability (and, as a necessary consequence, the composing skill, as well) but it is important to notice that they also, and inevitably, develop the reading ability at the same time. In the diagrams presented above, the unbroken lines indicate the linear sequence of statements and they show the path the reader follows at the immediate assimilation level of reading (see Chapter 3). The dotted lines indicate the underlying thematic development of the discourse and so represent the path the reader has to find at the discrimination level of reading. The writing exercises we have been discussing necessarily draw the learner's attention to the relationship between the support acts on the right of the diagrams and the main theme acts on the left and they can be seen as devices for developing the learner's awareness of the structure of discourse that he has to discover as he reads. In other words, these exercises further the underlying interpreting ability and are directed at an integration of different learning activities.

5.5.3 *Rhetorical transformation of discourse units*

We have seen how discourse units can be built up from simple acts by the use of exercises in rhetorical transformation. These have been represented as involving the sorting and appropriate combining of groups of statements from a randomly ordered set. But rhetorical transformation can also operate on units of discourse. Consider, for example, a structurally simple discourse unit like a set of directions for carrying out an experiment and a statement of its result. Such units occur very commonly in science textbooks. We can get the learner to construct such a unit from a set of randomly ordered acts and then to transform the unit into another of different communicative value. The following is an example of an exercise of this kind.

I Arrange the following statements in the right order:

Turn the glass upside down.
Take your hand away from the cardboard.
This shows that air exerts a pressure upwards.
Fill a glass to the brim with water.
The cardboard remains against the glass and the water remains in the glass.
Place a piece of cardboard over it.

II Change what you have written in Stage I to a description of the experiment.

Begin: A glass is filled . . .

If the learner carries out the transformation correctly he will produce the following simple description:

A glass is filled to the brim with water and a piece of cardboard placed over it. The glass is then turned upside down and the hand taken away from the cardboard. The cardboard remains against the glass and the water remains in the glass. This shows that air exerts a pressure upwards.

This unit of discourse can itself be subjected to transformation, of course. We might, for example, ask the learner to transform his description into a report. Note again that in doing these writing exercises the learner is necessarily also bringing his composing skill into operation. Writing a report based on the description given above, for example, requires him to produce correct past tense forms. But he cannot do so as an automatic composing task: the last statement, for example, which expresses a conclusion by reference to a general physical law, remains unchanged.

Another transformation that could be made here is one which converts the directions or the description or the report into a pair of statements expressing an observation and a conclusion. The result of such a transformation would be something like the following:

If a piece of cardboard is placed over a glass filled with water and the glass is then turned upside down, the cardboard will remain against the glass. This shows that air exerts a pressure upwards.

Alternatively, or in addition, the learner could be asked to produce a generalization + exemplification sequence of the kind that was discussed earlier:

Air exerts a pressure upwards. If, for example, a piece of cardboard is placed over a glass filled with water and the glass is then turned upside down, the cardboard will remain against the glass.

5.5.4 *Information transfer*

Earlier in this chapter, mention was made of the use that can be made of information transfer procedures in the design of writing exercises. It will be clear that the different kinds of discourse relating to the experiment about air pressure that we have been discussing lend themselves to procedures of this kind. We have spoken of the transformation of instances of discourse from one type into another but these instances of discourse can also be derived from a non-verbal mode of communicating. Thus, if we assume that the learner has the requisite knowledge of usage, we could ask him to write a set of directions and so on with reference to a non-verbal prompt in the form of a sequence of diagrams. This was suggesged as a possible procedure for preparation exercises earlier in this chapter. It will be convenient to repeat the point that was made then about exercises of this kind: they are comprehension questions of the information transfer type put, as it were, in reverse. Information transfer can work in two directions. When it is used to develop the reading ability the transfer is from the verbal to the non-verbal mode of communicating. When it is used to develop the writing ability, the transfer is from the non-verbal to the verbal mode of communicating. It is, therefore, a device for integrating these two abilities and for referring them to the common underlying process of interpreting.

But this is not only a feature of information transfer exercises. All of the exercises discussed in this and the preceding chapter provide for the possibility of relating the productive and receptive aspects of interpreting. In Chapter 4, for example, gradual approximation was introduced as a device for developing reading and in this chapter it was shown to be easily adaptable to the development of the writing ability. Similarly, the exercises in rhetorical transformation which have just been outlined clearly provide the learner with a knowledge of discourse development which he will bring to bear on his subsequent reading. In short, whether the emphasis is on reception or production, and obviously this emphasis will vary in different situations according to learner needs, exercises in use will necessarily relate to the underlying ability to interpret and will allow for the integration of reading and writing as aspects of that ability.

5.6 Summary and conclusion

Early in this chapter I made a distinction between preparation and exploitation exercises. I said that the first kind prepared the way for the reading passage and were therefore part of presentation, whereas the second kind drew their substance from the reading passage after it had been read and were therefore part of exploitation. But although one can make this distinction with reference to the positioning of different exercises in relation to a particular reading passage, the effectiveness of such exercises as elements in a cyclical process depends on our avoiding any real functional distinction. The kind of exercises that have been discussed in the latter part of this chapter are of an exploitation kind in the sense that they may exploit aspects of usage and use introduced in a preceding reading passage. But they are preparatory in the sense that they prepare the learner for his encounter with instances of discourse of a similar sort: in exploiting one passage, they prepare for the next.

My procedure in this chapter has been very much the same as that which I adopted in the last. I first tried to give systematic consideration to certain common types of exercise and then explored a number of alternative ways of proceeding, ways which attempted to cast the notions introduced in the first part of the book into practical pedagogic form. The arguments I have presented and their working out in practice leads us, it seems to me, to the conclusion that the effective teaching of language as communication calls for an integrated approach which represents different skills and abilities as aspects of a singly underlying activity. The exercises proposed in the last two chapters do, I think, provide some exemplification of such an approach. In the chapter that follows (the last) I want to try to assemble the observations that have been made and the illustrations that have been given into a simple methodological scheme.

Notes and references

1. See Note 2, Chapter 4.
2. It is for this reason that linguists have had difficulties in eliciting from informants judgements about the correctness of sentences presented in isolation. Informants will tend to assess the use potential of sentences by relating them to possible contexts. The same sort of thing happens when informants are asked to give the meaning of lexical items: they tend to provide them with a value in context rather than to define their signification. It is natural to consider language as use and it takes some effort of disorientation to treat it as usage.
3. This passage, though not the treatment of it given here, appears in modified form in:
   J. P. B. Allen & H. G. Widdowson: *English in Social Studies*, Oxford University Press, 1978. This is a title in the *English in Focus* series.
4. This example is taken from another title in the *English in Focus* series:
   Eric H. Glendinning: *English in Mechanical Engineering*, 1975.
5. This exercise again is a modification of one to be found in *English in Mechanical Engineering*.
6. One of the maxims mentioned by Grice as subsumed under the general co-operative principle (see Note 4, Chapter 2) is that the speaker (or writer) will not make a statement which he believes to be false or for which he cannot provide sufficient evidence.
7. In fact, the lack is, in some respects, being remedied. There is a good deal of work going on at the moment into the communicative functioning of language and this is now being incorporated into pedagogic descriptions. See for example:
   Geoffrey Leech & Jan Svartvik: *A Communicative Grammar of English*, Longman, 1975.
   J. A. Van Ek: *The Threshold Level*, Council of Europe, 1975.

6 Towards an integrated approach

6.1 Preview: the need for integration

It was suggested at the end of the last chapter that the teaching of language as communication calls for an approach which brings linguistic skills and communicative abilities into close association with each other. We have seen that even though a particular exercise may focus on a particular skill or ability, its effectiveness will often require the learner to make reference to other aspects of his communicative competence.[1] That this should be so is consistent with the scheme of skills and abilities presented in Chapter 3, in which (it will be recalled) all linguistic behaviour was related to the underlying activity of interpreting. It is not surprising that this relationship should assert itself through the design and execution of language learning exercises directed at the development of the ability to handle use. In this book I have represented the learner's task as essentially one which involves acquiring a communicative competence in the language, that is to say, an ability to interpret discourse, whether the emphasis is on productive or receptive behaviour. If this definition of the learner's aim is accepted, it would seem to follow that any approach directed at achieving it should avoid treating the different skills and abilities that constitute competence in isolation from each other, as ends in themselves. What the learner needs to know how to do is to compose in the act of writing, comprehend in the act of reading, and to learn techniques of reading by writing and techniques of writing by reading. If the aim of language learning is to develop the underlying interpreting ability, then it would seem reasonable to adopt an integrated approach to achieve it.

But conventional pedagogic practice has tended to move in the opposite direction. The basic principle appears to be an adherence to segregation rather than integration: 'divide and rule'.[2] As was pointed out earlier, language teaching courses commonly consist of units in which 'comprehension', 'grammar' and 'composition' appear as separate sections, and language practice books tend to be based on the same distinctions. It is frequently the case that the different sections of the basic formula in course books have no principled connection with each other. Indeed, there is often considerable disparity between the different sections. Thus, it is not unusual to find grammar exercises providing practice in areas of usage which the reading passage and comprehension questions have already presupposed a knowledge of and which the learner must himself bring to bear in answering the questions. Again, one frequently finds that the composition section makes much greater demands on the learner than the grammar section has prepared him to meet. The grammar exercises may, for example, require the learner to carry out elementary completion, conversion and transformation operations on single and isolated sentences and these might be followed without further warning or preparation by an exercise which requires the learner to write a short essay or a summary of the passage he has read. In cases like this, the grammar exercises, focussed as they are on usage, provide only a very partial and inadequate preparation for such a complex writing task.

I do not want to suggest that all language teaching material in current circulation suffers from the kind of division I have described. The kind of basic formula that I have outlined is more in the nature of a conventional norm towards which materials tend to approximate. I have used it as a convenient starting point for discussion but it is important to recognize that a good deal of work has been done which does not subscribe to the attitude it implies. The teaching of language as communication has been going on for some time in some quarters[3] and all I can claim in this respect is that I might have clarified certain principles in this book which already inform pedagogic practice. I think it is important to recognize also that a good deal of material developed along conventional lines has yielded impressive results and from that point of view I would wish to represent the approach outlined in this book as a development from previous work, an attempt to re-align existing ideas and practices so as to make them more effective. In the previous two chapters I have subjected some of these ideas and practices to fairly close scrutiny and I have suggested ways in which the principles which appear to underlie them might be made more explicit and might be modified to account for the teaching of use. What I want to do in this final chapter is to reduce this previous discussion to a set of basic proposals representing an outline scheme for an integrated approach.

6.2 The discourse-to-discourse scheme

Since our aim is to get the learner to cope with discourse in one way or another, it would seem reasonable to suggest that instances of discourse should serve as the point of reference for all the exercises which are devised. I would like to propose that teaching units and the teaching tasks they specify should be organized as moves from one instance of discourse to another. The first of these constitutes the reading passage, which can be prepared for by the kind of procedures outlined in Chapter 4. The second instance of discourse is created by the learner himself by reference to the first and all of the exercises which intervene between the two are designed to formulate this reference in a controlled way and to help the learner thereby to transfer his interpreting from its receptive realization as reading to its productive realization as writing. Each exercise, therefore, is justified by its effectiveness as a stage in the learner's progress from the first instance of discourse to the second. So the progress is conceived of as cyclical: the exploitation of the first instance of discourse has at the same time the function of preparing the learner for his production of the second. The focus of attention thus gradually shifts from the interpreting of discourse in reading to the interpreting of discourse in writing. The function of the exercises is to mediate this shift. We might express this process in terms of a simple diagram:

interpreting

reading   writing

discourse 1 . . . (exercises) . . . > discourse 2

6.3   Types of procedure

We now have to consider what kind of exercises we need to effect the transition from discourse 1 to discourse 2. A number of likely candidates have already been proposed in the course of the previous chapters and what I want to do now is to relate them to two main types of procedure. These have also been referred to earlier. They are rhetorical transformation and information transfer.

As we have seen in the preceding chapter, rhetorical transformation may involve the writing of an instance of discourse through the process of gradual approximation beginning with sentences or rhetorical acts as primary units. Alternatively it may involve the derivation of one instance of discourse from another, a complete shift in communicative value. We can, for convenience of reference, refer to this second operation as one of illocutionary change. Thus, for example, the rhetorical transformation of a set of directions into a description, such as was illustrated in the preceding chapter, is an example of illocutionary change.

6.3.1   *Demonstration: rhetorical transformation by gradual approximation*
Let us examine the use of the gradual approximation procedure first.

Let us suppose that after having been primed by the kind of preparatory exercise considered in the preceding chapter, the learner is presented with the following reading passage:[4]

Discourse 1. [1]Some liquids which act as conductors of electricity decompose when an electric current is passed through them. [2]Such liquids, usually solutions of certain chemicals in water, are known as electrolytes. [3]The process by which they are decomposed is called electrolysis. [4]In electrolysis, two wires or pieces of metal connected to a battery or cell are placed in a vessel containing an electrolyte. [5]These are called electrodes. [6]The electrode connected to the negative terminal of the battery is called the cathode and that which is connected to the positive terminal is called the anode.

[7]When the current is switched on, it passes from the battery to the anode and then through the electrolyte to the cathode, passing from there back to the battery. [8]As the current passes from one electrode to the other a chemical reaction takes place.

The first step is to exploit this passage by means of the kind of exercises discussed in Chapter 4: interpretation checks, which focus on the reading ability, and related explanatory solutions which engage the learner's composing skill as a part of the making of statements with a bearing on the passage. Interpretation checks and explanatory solutions might in this case take the following form:

Interpretation checks

(a) Liquids which decompose when an electric current passes through them are called electrolytes.
(b) Electrolytes are solutions of certain chemicals in water.
(c) A chemical reaction takes place when an electric current passes through an electrolyte.

Explanatory solutions

(a) Some liquids decompose when an electric current . . . (1) through them.
   Such liquids are . . . (3) electrolytes.
i.e. Liquids which . . . (1) when an electric current is passed through them are . . . (2) as electrolytes.
= Liquids which decompose when an electric current passes through them are called electrolytes.

(b) Liquids which decompose when . . . (1) passes through them are usually solutions of certain chemicals in water.
i.e. . . . (2) are . . . (2) solutions of certain chemicals in water.
i.e. Electrolytes are not *always* solutions of certain chemicals in water.

(c) When the electric current passes from one . . . (8) to the other, a chemical reaction takes place.

i.e. When the electric current passes from the . . . (7) to the . . . (8) a chemical reaction takes place.

When the current passes from anode to cathode, it passes through the . . . (7)

∴ A chemical reaction takes place when an electric current passes through the electrolyte.

The completion of these explanatory solutions is not, in this particular case, a very demanding task but it can, of course, be adjusted for difficulty as required. The purpose of such an exercise is to get the learner to look closely at how meaning is conveyed in the passage, to draw his attention to features of cohesion and coherence by actively engaging him in the rational reformulation of meanings. The learner participates in the completion of a coherent argument based on what is said in the passage. In this way his task is provided with a communicative significance. The next step might then be to introduce an exercise which increased the demand on the composing skill while still involving interpretative reference to the reading passage. Something like the following transformation exercise might serve the purpose:

Exercise 1

With reference to the passage, combine the following groups of sentences so that they make appropriate statements:

(a) Some liquids act as conductors of electricity.
Some liquids decompose when an electric current passes through them.

(b) The vessel contains an electrolyte.
In this process, two pieces of metal are connected to a battery.
In this process, two pieces of metal are placed in a vessel.

(c) One electrode is connected to the positive terminal of the battery.
One electrode is connected to the negative terminal of the battery.
One electrode is called the cathode.
One electrode is called the anode.

(d) A chemical reaction takes place.
The current is switched on.
The current passes through the electrolyte.

Notice again that although this exercise makes demands on the learner's composing skill, he does not apply it simply for its own sake but in order to make meaningful statements: it is brought into operation as a necessary aspect of writing. The four sentences in (c), for example, can be combined in such a way as to compose the following sentence:

One electrode, which is called the anode, is connected to the negative terminal of the battery and the other electrode, which is called the cathode, is connected to the positive terminal of the battery.

But although this is impeccably correct as a sentence, it is not correct as a statement about anodes and cathodes. Similarly, it is possible to combine the sentence in (d) to form a sentence which is correct but a statement which is inaccurate:

When a chemical reaction takes place, the current is switched on and passes through the electrolyte.

This transformation exercise already takes the learner some way towards discourse by providing him with the opportunity to make use of anaphoric items like *the other* (in (c)) and *it* (in (d)). The next step might move him further in this direction by requiring him to take the sentences he has produced and combine them with other sentences derived from the original passage. By doing this the learner arrives at a second instance of discourse which is a summary version of the first.

Exercise 2

Combine the following sentences with the sentences you have written in Exercise 1 to make a summary of the reading passage. Change the sentences where necessary:

(a) The pieces of metal connected to a battery are known as electrodes.
(b) The process by which some liquids decompose when an electric current passes through them is called electrolysis.
(c) Liquids which decompose when an electric current passes through them are known as electrolytes.
(d) The current passes from one electrode to the other.

One possible output from these operations is the following:

Discourse 2. Some liquids which act as conductors of electricity decompose when an electric current passes through them. Such liquids are known as electrolytes and the process is called electrolysis. In this process, two pieces of metal, known as electrodes, are connected to a battery and placed in a vessel containing an electrolyte. One electrode, called the cathode, is connected to the negative terminal and the other, called the anode, to the positive terminal of the battery. When the current is switched on, it passes through the electrolyte from one electrode to the other and a chemical reaction takes place.

This is not, of course, the only possible version. To the extent that other versions are possible, this exercise has an element of free composition, but as a piece of writing it is constrained by the communicative purpose which derives from the original passage. Two further observations might be made. Firstly, it will be noticed that the version that has been given exemplifies a number of contracted relative clauses. It may be that an additional transformation exercise would need to be included to give learners practice in this aspect of grammar. But such an exercise would again not be conducted as an independent operation but would be linked up with the other exercises as a step towards the ultimate writing of a second instance of discourse. In this way, the learner can be made aware of the communicative purpose of such an exercise. The second observation that might be made is this: as was noted earlier in this chapter (and in Chapter 5), writing exercises, including the writing of summaries, are very often given to the learner without adequate preparation, as a separate task. The kind of approach demonstrated here indicates how the learner can be guided through gradual approximation to summary writing and how it can represent an interpretative output resulting from an integration of skills and abilities.

The example of gradual approximation we have just considered yields a second instance of discourse which is a *restatement* of the first. We can make use of the same procedure to produce an instance of discourse which is a *continuation* of the first. We can do this by first introducing a modified version of our Exercise 1:

*Exercise 1*a

Complete the following sentences by writing in the correct form of the verb in brackets and then combine them to make appropriate statements:

(a) The vessel (contain) an electrolyte.
    Two pieces of metal (connect) to a battery.
    Two pieces of metal (place) in a vessel.
(b) The beaker (contain) blue copper sulphate solution.
    Two pieces of platinum foil (connect) to a battery.
    Two pieces of platinum foil (place) in a beaker.
(c) One electrode (connect) to the positive terminal of the battery.
    One electrode (connect) to the negative terminal of the battery.
    One electrode (call) the cathode.
    One electrode (call) the anode.
(d) One piece of platinum foil (connect) to the negative terminal of the battery.
    One piece of platinum foil (connect) to the positive terminal of the battery.
(e) A test tube (fill) with copper sulphate solution.
    A test tube (fix) over the anode.

(f) A chemical reaction (take) place.
   The current (switch on).
   The current (pass) through the electrolyte.
(g) The blue copper sulphate solution gradually (become) paler.
   The current (pass) through the blue copper sulphate solution.
(h) The current (switch on).
   The current (pass) through the copper sulphate solution.
   The current (pass) from anode to cathode.
(i) Gas (give off) from the anode.
   Gas (collect) in the test tube.

This exercise is intended to achieve a number of ends. Firstly, the learner will be given composing practice in providing correct verb forms. The reading passage will give him guidance in completing those sentences which derive from it and this guidance will in turn transfer to his completion of those sentences which do not relate to the passage. Secondly, the learner will be producing two sets of combined sentences in parallel. Those resulting from (a), (c) and (f) can be related to the reading passage whereas those resulting from (b), (d), (e), (g), (h) and (i) cannot. But the 'new' sentences are structurally similar to those which are 'given' so that the way in which they are combined is linked to the reading passage through the 'given' sentences. Thirdly, this link with the reading passage realizes an illocutionary significance. The 'new' sentences clearly represent particular instances of what is described in the 'given' sentences: the structural similarity is symptomatic of a related illocutionary function. The next step is to move the learner towards the writing of a complete unit of discourse which will realize this communicative function to the full. A variant of Exercise 2 can be used for this purpose:

Exercise 2[a]
Combine the following sentences with the sentences you have written in Exercise 1[a] (b), (d), (e) and (g) to make a paragraph which is a continuation of the reading passage. Change the sentences where necessary:

(a) The copper sulphate solution gets paler.
(b) The copper sulphate solution is decomposed by the electric current.
(c) The electric current passes through the copper sulphate solution.
(d) Let us see what happens when platinum electrodes are used with an electrolyte of copper sulphate solution.

In performing these operations, the learner is led to see that in order to construct an appropriate paragraph, the sentence resulting from a combination of (a), (b) and (c) must be placed at the end where it will serve as an explanation of what is described in the sentence emerging from

Exercise 1ª (g). He will also be made aware that sentence (d) in Exercise 2ª must come first in the paragraph to effect the necessary connection with the reading passage, and to indicate that the paragraph he is constructing expresses a particular example of the general description of electrolysis given in the original passage. In short, he is led to an awareness of the discourse value of the text he is constructing. The output of this exercise, then, is a second instance of discourse:

Discourse 2ª   Let us see what happens when platinum electrodes are used with an electrolyte of copper sulphate solution. Two pieces of platinum foil are connected to a battery and placed in a beaker containing blue copper sulphate solution. One piece is connected to the positive terminal and the other to the negative terminal of the battery. A test tube is filled with the solution and fixed over the anode. When the current is switched on, it passes from anode to cathode through the solution. Gas is given off from the anode and is collected in the test tube. The blue copper sulphate solution gradually becomes paler as the current passes through it. It gets paler because it is decomposed by the current.

Again, this is not the only possible version and again we have a degree of freedom of composition constrained by the communicative purpose that the completed paragraph must serve as an illustrative paragraph following on from the original reading passage.

A number of refinements and variations could be introduced into the exercise material, and indeed would probably have to be introduced to meet the requirements of individual groups of learners, but the foregoing examples perhaps provide sufficient demonstration of the possibilities of the gradual approximation process as a way of integrating exercises which are analytic with reference to one instance of discourse and synthetic with reference to a second and so effect a transition from one to the other.

6.3.2   *Demonstration: rhetorical transformation by illocutionary change*
Let us now turn our attention to illocutionary change. The description of the process of electrolysis provided in Discourse 1 gives information which can be used for the drawing up of a set of directions for carrying out the process described. That is to say, the propositional content of the passage can be recast into a different communicative form so that it has a different illocutionary value. As a first step towards this change we might require the learner to demonstrate that he has read the passage with understanding by arranging a set of directions in the correct sequence. The following exercise might be devised for that purpose:

Exercise 3

Put the following sentences in an order which shows the correct sequence of directions for carrying out the experiment described in the passage. Change the sentences where necessary:

(a) Fill a vessel with electrolyte.
(b) Place two pieces of metal in a vessel.
(c) Connect two pieces of metal to a battery.
(d) Switch on the current.

Note that we could, if we wished, add a further composing requirement to our exercise by presenting not complete sentences but abbreviated forms of directions like the following:

Exercise 3ᵃ

Write out the following as complete sentences and then put them in an order which shows the correct sequence of directions for carrying out the experiment described in the passage. Change the sentences where necessary:

(a) Fill vessel—electrolyte.
(b) Place two pieces metal in vessel.
(c) Connect two pieces metal—battery.
(d) Switch on current.

In doing this exercise, the learner transforms the description in the passage to a set of directions. We now want him to move towards the production of a second instance of discourse related to the one presented as the reading passage. We can do this by providing a second set of directions related to the first and arranged in the correct order or not (depending on the degree of difficulty required) and by asking the learner to change these directions into a description. The description in Discourse 1 will, of course, serve as a model.

Exercise 4

Change the following set of directions into a description:

(a) Connect two pieces of platinum foil to a battery.
(b) Fill a beaker with blue copper sulphate solution.
(c) Fill a test tube with the solution.
(d) Connect one piece of metal to the negative terminal.
(e) Connect one piece of metal to the positive terminal.
(f) Fix the test tube over the anode.
(g) Place the two pieces of platinum foil in the beaker.
(h) Switch on the current.

(In this case, it will be noted, the directions are *not* in the right order.)

The result of this exercise is a second instance of discourse which relates to part of Discourse 1: essentially it represents a particular example of the general process described in Discourse 1, which therefore provides a good model for the learner's guidance. But since the discourse resulting from Exercise 4 *is* a particular instance of the general process, it can be developed into a continuation of Discourse 1. So we might now introduce a variant of Exercise 2 along something like the following lines:

Exercise 5
Combine the following sentences with the description you have made in Exercise 4 so as to write a paragraph which is a continuation of the reading passage. Change the sentences where necessary:

(a) The current passes from anode to cathode through the solution.
(b) Let us consider what happens when platinum electrodes are used with an electrolyte of copper sulphate solution.
(c) The current passes through the solution.
(d) The solution gradually becomes paler.
(e) Gas is given off from the anode.
(f) Gas is collected in the test tube.
(g) The blue copper sulphate solution gets paler.
(h) The copper sulphate solution is decomposed.
(i) The current passes through the copper sulphate solution.

The product of this exercise will be a version of Discourse 2a.

I have tried to demonstrate how rhetorical transformation works as a set of procedures for deriving one instance of discourse from another by means of controlled and purposeful language practice. This derivation can occur through gradual approximation or through illocutionary change, or indeed by a combination of these. The demonstration I have given of these procedures has necessarily been brief and simplified. It should be noted that the steps in the derivation for particular groups of learners might call for more mediating exercises than I have given here. It may be necessary, for example, to provide exercises on certain troublesome points of grammar or on particular aspects of cohesion or on the coherent development of particular rhetorical acts. What I have tried to indicate here is a teaching strategy: the tactical manoeuvres required to put this into practice in different circumstances must ultimately be a matter for the individual teacher's judgement of learner needs. The same point must be made about the second main procedure to be discussed, information transfer, to which I now turn.

6.3.3 *Demonstration: information transfer*
Whereas rhetorical transformation is an operation on the verbal aspects

of discourse, information transfer is an operation on its non-verbal aspects as well. It has been pointed out a number of times in this book that if we are seriously interested in the teaching of language as communication, then we cannot ignore the fact that communication is not restricted to verbal textualization. A good deal of written discourse makes use of non-verbal modes of communicating and an understanding of how these function in association with the verbal text is often crucial for interpretation. Among what we will call non-verbal representations in written discourse are maps, charts, diagrams, formulae and graphs and these have to be read as well in the interpreting of the discourse as a whole. What the information transfer procedure does is to use such non-verbal representations as a way of mediating a transition from one discourse to another.

This is how the procedure works. The learner is presented with an instance of discourse, a reading passage for which he is primed by the kind of preparation exercises discussed in Chapter 4, and he is required to carry out an interpretation exercise involving the use of a non-verbal representation of the information expressed in the passage. A second instance of non-verbal representation, similar in certain respects to the first, is then presented and the learner is required to derive a second instance of discourse from it. The first stage, then is an interpretation exercise of the information transfer type such as was referred to in Chapter 4 and the second stage is a writing exercise which reverses the process of transfer from non-verbal to verbal representation. We can illustrate this by reference to our passage on electrolysis:

Discourse 1 (teacher's input)

Some liquids which act as conductors of electricity . . . etc . . . . . .
. . . . As the current passes from one electrode to the other a chemical reaction takes place.

Exercise 6   (*Non-verbal representation 1*)

Label the diagram and
indicate with arrows
the direction of the
current.

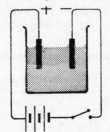

Exercise 7

Write a description illustrating the process of electrolysis by reference to the diagram.

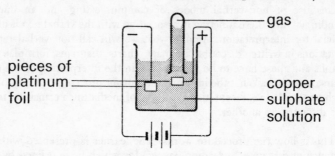

(*Non-verbal representation 2*)

Discourse 2 (learner's output)

Two pieces of platinum foil are connected to a battery and placed in a beaker containing copper sulphate solution . . . etc . . . .
. . . . Gas is given off from the anode and is collected in the test tube.

Both information transfer and rhetorical transformation exercises aim at getting the learner to write something based on his reading and so to represent these two abilities as aspects of the same underlying interpreting process. The two kinds of exercise are different in certain respects. With rhetorical transformation, for example, there is a greater emphasis on composing and more overt analysis of the first instance of discourse, particularly with respect to gradual approximation exercises. As the name suggests, gradual approximation involves a controlled move from an analysis of Discourse 1 to a synthesis of Discourse 2, so that the exercises are both preparation and exploitation at the same time. Illocutionary change represents the transition from one discourse to another more directly, at the same level of rhetorical structure and in this respect it resembles information transfer. It might be helpful if I were to give my own non-verbal representation of those different procedures.

Rhetorical transformation

(a) *Gradual approximation:*

analysis   synthesis

Discourse 1 . . . . exercises . . . . → Discourse 2

(b) *Illocutionary change:*

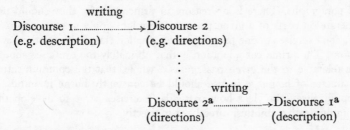

Information transfer

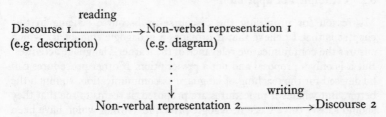

It is important to note that although for the convenience of exposition I have dealt with those procedures separately, they can be used together to complement each other. Thus, for example, gradual approximation exercises can be used in the transition from Discourse 1 to Discourse 2 in the illocutionary change procedure. Again, illocutionary change and information transfer can take place concurrently. In which case, we might get the following scheme:

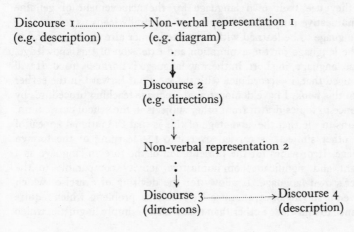

Another point that might be noted is that these procedures need not only apply to large discourse units, to passages consisting of a number of paragraphs. There is no reason, in principle, why they should not operate on parts of a given passage: we might apply gradual approximation exercises to one paragraph, information transfer to another, and so on. The prime consideration is that ultimately the exercises should be relatable to the given passage as a whole, that the communicative character of language in use should be constantly borne in mind. It should always be clear how particular exercises serve to develop the communicative abilities, directly or indirectly.

6.4   Principles of approach

My reason for proposing the discourse-to-discourse scheme in this chapter is that I believe that it provides a pedagogic framework which ensures the communicative relevance of the learner's language activities. But it is only a proposal and not a prescription. If other procedures can be devised for the teaching of language as communication, so much the better. But whatever procedures are proposed, it seems to me that they should satisfy three basic pedagogic principles, two of which have been mentioned previously as following naturally from the discussion in the first part of this book. They are: the principle of rational appeal, the principle of integration, and the principle of control.

6.4.1   *Rational appeal: the use of translation*

What is meant by the first of these is that language learners should be made aware of what they are doing when they undertake language tasks, that they should be led to recognize that these tasks relate to the way they use their own language for the achievement of genuine communicative purposes. This principle naturally leads us to associate the language to be learned with what the learner already knows and to use the language for the exploration and extension of this knowledge. To use language, in short, in the way language is normally used. It will be noticed that, in accordance with the view put forward in the earlier part of this book, I have demonstrated language teaching procedures by reference to topics drawn from other subjects in the school curriculum. It seems to me that the advantage of this is that the rational appeal of these other subjects is carried over into the learning of the foreign language. It provides for the presentation of the foreign language as a relevant and significant communicative activity comparable to the learner's own language. It allows for the devising of exercises which involve the solving of communicative problems, problems which require reference to knowledge other than that which is simply linguistic, which make demands on the linguistic skills only to the extent that they are an intrinsic feature of communicative abilities.

I have spoken of the principle of rational appeal as applying to the association of the language being learned with areas of non-linguistic knowledge so that the learner knows what he is doing and why he is doing it. The principle might also be applied to the association of the language being learned with the language the learner already knows. What we are aiming to do is to make the learner conceive of the foreign language in the same way as he conceives of his own language and to use it in the same way as communicative activity. This being so, it would seem reasonable to draw upon the learner's knowledge of how his own language is used to communicate. That is to say, it would seem reasonable to make use of translation.

Exercises in translation can easily be accommodated within the discourse-to-discourse schemes that have been proposed. Exercises 1 and 2 on our passage on electrolysis for example could present L1 as well as L2 sentences related to the passage, and we could have a parallel development of two instances of discourse by gradual approximation: one in the L1 and the other in the L2. We might diagrammize such a procedure as follows:

$$\text{Discourse 1} \ldots\ldots\ldots\ldots\text{exercises} \begin{cases} \longrightarrow \text{Discourse 2 (L1)} \\ \longrightarrow \text{Discourse 3 (L2)} \end{cases}$$

Another possibility is that we could introduce exercises in illocutionary change operating on individual acts in both L1 and L2, thus drawing the learner's attention to the way in which these acts are differently realized in the two languages. An exercise of this type could be included in a gradual approximation sequence, or could be developed to derive an instance of discourse in the L1 from an instance of discourse in the L2, or the reverse. In the latter case the discourse-to-discourse derivation through illocutionary change might take the following form:

Discourse 1 (L2)..................→Discourse 2 (L2)
(e.g. description)   (e.g. directions)

.
.
.
↓

Discourse 2ª (L1)...........→ Discourse 1ª (L1)
(directions)   (description)

Translation exercises might also be introduced into the information transfer procedure. We could relate the first non-verbal representation, for example, to two instances of discourse in parallel, one in the L1 and the other in the L2 and require two instances of discourse as output. Such an information transfer procedure would look like this:

Discourse 1 (L1)
                   ↘ Non-verbal representation 1
Discourse 1ᵃ (L2) ↗   (e.g. diagram)
(e.g. description)   .

                               .

                               .

                       ↓   ↗ Discourse 2 (L1)
              Non-verbal representation 2
                                                   ↘ Discourse 2ᵃ (L2)

Notice that the incorporation of translation into these procedures ensures that it is carried out as a communicative activity. Their purpose is to make clear to the learner just what is involved in such activity by relating it to his own experience of language. Translation here, then, is an operation on language use and not simply on language usage and aims at making the learner aware of the communicative value of the language he is learning by overt reference to the communicative functioning of his own language.

6.4.2   Integration and control

The principle of integration has already been discussed in some detail and the ways in which the procedures I have suggested exemplify it are, I hope, apparent and need no further commentary. There is one point, however, which perhaps stands in need of further clarification. The kind of exercises which I have suggested involve the learner in the production of written work. But the question might arise: are they then appropriate for learners whose principal purpose in learning the language is to acquire study skills in reading? Furthermore, is there not a danger that the learners' development in reading might be held back by engaging him in the more difficult and time-consuming activity of writing? Questions of this kind have been raised in connection with the traditional practice in language teaching of tying reading activities in with oral practice on the one hand and exercises in sentence construction on the other. And it is indeed not easy to see the justification for imposing a dependency on different skills in this way. But the dependency that the proposed procedures in this book seek to establish and exploit is that which relates different communicative abilities. The view put forward in Chapter 3 is that the abilities of reading and writing are alternative realizations of the same underlying interpreting ability and it is this which the exercises that have been suggested are meant to develop. In this view, the activity of writing makes overt strategies of interpretation which the practised language user brings to bear when he reads. The written work required of the learner in the proposed exercises, therefore, is a means of getting him to participate in the development of a general ability which underlies reading.

The point about learner participation brings us to the principle of control. Traditionally the control on the language learning process has been achieved by strict limits imposed on the input. Thus language data is gradually filtered through to the learner by careful selection and grading so that he is exposed to very little language at a time. With this kind of control, it is very difficult for the language to be anything else but instances of usage. The filtering process must of necessity make it extremely difficult for the learner to respond to the language in an authentic way and in presenting small bits of language data at a time to the learner one is bound to be representing the language he is to learn as something quite different from the language he has already learned as a mother tongue. This kind of control puts foreign language learning at a remove from the learner's previous experience of language.

But there is an alternative means of achieving control. Instead of controlling the input we can control the intake. That is to say, instead of restricting the amount of language to which the learner is exposed we restrict the amount of attention that the learner pays to what he is exposed to. We do this by limiting the kind of interpretation task the learner is required to undertake. The advantage of this kind of control is that it is a normal feature of communicative behaviour whereas control by limiting exposure is not. When we listen to talk or read something we are able to adjust our attention: the input is one thing, but our intake is another. We in fact impose our own filter on the data.

The kind of procedures that have been put forward in this book allow for the controlled intake of data. The learner is exposed to an instance of discourse and then his attention is drawn to particular aspects of it in the exercises which follow. There is no requirement that he should understand every word. In the information transfer exercises, for example, the non-verbal representation may in fact relate to only one part of the unit of discourse to which the learner is exposed and part of his task is to ignore those features of the discourse which are not relevant to his task in completing the non-verbal representation. The difficulty of the task is also controlled by regulating the amount of information which the learner needs to complete it. Thus instead of restricting the learner to elementary tasks which might seem to lie within his linguistic competence but which are plainly incongruously simple in relation to his intellectual capacity in general, we control the contribution which the learner must make to the completion of more complex tasks. The non-verbal representation related to a reading passage might, for example, be quite a complicated diagram, or graph, one which would genuinely appear in the kind of discourse from which the reading passage derives. Now if the passage is thought to be too difficult for the learner to process unaided in his search for relevant information, then part of this information can be provided. For example, the diagram can be partially labelled, the graph partially completed. In this way we try to approximate to a normal exposure to language and a normal involvement in communicative activity. We try, in short, to set up the right conditions for an authentic response.

6.5   Summary and conclusion

I have spent some time demonstrating how the procedures that have been proposed in this book put into practice the three principles of rational appeal, integration and control. I do not wish to imply that these are the only procedures which can put these principles into practice, nor indeed that these are the only principles with which we as language teachers should be concerned. In this book I have tried to develop a rational approach to the teaching of language as communication based on a careful consideration of the nature of language and of the language user's activities. It may be that many of my conclusions will turn out to be mistaken in the light of actual teaching experience and in the light of further enquiry into the communicative functioning of language. It should be stressed, with reference to the first point, that what I have proposed here is speculative and its validity is subject to the test of practical application. With reference to the second point, it must be stressed that the study of language use is still in its early stages: we know very little at present about such matters as the way discourse develops and the way different rhetorical activities are to be characterized. There is no source of reference for the teaching of use as there is for the teaching of usage. In these circumstances, it is prudent not to be too positive in one's recommendations.

At the same time I think it would be a mistake to be too timorous. Our lack of certainty about how language is put to communicative use might incline us to the view that we should wait for more definitive findings to emerge from research before we adopt a communicative orientation to the teaching of language. I think that this would be an unfortunate view to take. It would imply that language teachers are simply consumers of other people's products, that they are incapable of initiative and must only make advances in methodology across ground already prepared by proclaimed theorists. But the language teacher need not, and usually does not, assume such a passive role. He can, and does, conduct operational research and he is in the position of being able to explore the possibilities of a communicative approach to teaching for himself. What I have tried to do in this book is to suggest some possibilities that might be explored.

Language teachers are often represented, by themselves and others, as humble practitioners, essentially practical people concerned with basic classroom tactics and impatient of theory. Such a representation is unnecessarily demeaning. Of course the teacher is concerned with practical results, but his practice is based on theoretical notions, no matter how inexplicit they may be. To repeat what I said at the end of Chapter 3, I think that it is important to recognize that language teaching is a theoretical as well as a practical occupation. Teaching techniques and materials must ultimately be related to underlying principles. It has been my concern in this book to enquire into principles and to explore their implications for the teaching of language as communication. If it provokes teachers into a systematic investigation of the ideas that inform their own practices, and stimulates them to enquire into the pedagogic possibilities of other ideas, then it will have achieved its object.

Notes and references

1. The term 'communicative competence' is now very much in fashion and for this reason alone it is as well to be wary of it: particularly since it does not always seem to be used in the same sense by different writers. It should be noted that if (as here) it is meant to refer to the knowledge of how the language system is realized as use in social contexts, then it *includes* competence in the more restricted Chomskyan sense of that term (see Note *1*, Chapter 1). For a discussion of the notion of communicative competence see: J. P. B. Allen & H. G. Widdowson, 'Grammar and language teaching' in *ECAL, Volume 2*, and the references cited there.

2. It should be noted, however, that over recent years a good deal of material has been written which has an integrative aim. Mention should be made, for example, of the materials written by L. G. Alexander under the general heading of *New Concept English* (Longman), which are referred to on the cover as 'integrated courses'. The integration, however, is applied to linguistic skills rather than to communicative abilities, as these have been defined in Chapter 3. The difference between Alexander's view of language learning (at that time) and that which has been proposed in this book can be seen from the following quotation:

'In order to become a skilled performer, the student must become proficient at using the units of a language. And the unit of a language is not, as was once commonly supposed, the word, but the sentence. Learning words irrespective of their function can be a waste of time . . .', *Practice and Progress*, 1967, p. vii.

I would say that learning sentences irrespective of their function can also be a waste of time.

It is also worth noting that although the courses are represented as integrated ones, the learning tasks are defined in a way which suggests that the skills are still thought of as quite separate kinds of activity.

'The student must be trained adequately in all four basic language skills: *understanding, speaking, reading* and *writing* . . . The following order of presentation must be taken as axiomatic;
> Nothing should be spoken before it has been heard.
> Nothing should be read before it has been spoken.
> Nothing should be written before it has been read.'

Practice and Progress, p. viii

3. Mention might be made, for example, of the work done by C. N. Candlin and his associates at the University of Lancaster on the development of English courses for overseas doctors and courses in study skills in English for overseas students. This work is described in Christopher N. Candlin, J. Michael Kirkwood & Helen M. Moore: 'Developing study skills in English' in *English for Academic Study*, ETIC Occasional Paper, The British Council, 1975.

   Considerable work is also going on at the University of Reading Centre for Applied Language Studies under its director D. A. Wilkins. Two of Wilkins' colleagues, Keith Johnson and Keith Morrow, have produced an experimental course which has a title which openly proclaims its pedagogic orientation: *Communicate*.

   Mention might also be made of:

   Martin Bates & Tony Dudley-Evans: *Nucleus: English for Science and Technology: General Science*, Longmans, 1976.

4. This passage appears in the *English in Focus* title *English in Physical Science*.

Index